Cambridge Elements

Elements in Critical Issues in Teacher Education
edited by
Tony Loughland
University of New South Wales
Andy Gao
University of New South Wales
Hoa T. M. Nguyen
University of New South Wales

DECOLONIZING PEDAGOGY IN POST-APARTHEID SOUTH AFRICA

A Post-Vygotskian Ethicopolitical and Ontoepistemic Postulation

Azwihangwisi Edward Muthivhi
University of Pretoria

Shaftesbury Road, Cambridge CB2 8EA, United Kingdom

One Liberty Plaza, 20th Floor, New York, NY 10006, USA

477 Williamstown Road, Port Melbourne, VIC 3207, Australia

314–321, 3rd Floor, Plot 3, Splendor Forum, Jasola District Centre, New Delhi – 110025, India

103 Penang Road, #05–06/07, Visioncrest Commercial, Singapore 238467

Cambridge University Press is part of Cambridge University Press & Assessment, a department of the University of Cambridge.

We share the University's mission to contribute to society through the pursuit of education, learning and research at the highest international levels of excellence.

www.cambridge.org
Information on this title: www.cambridge.org/9781009482561

DOI: 10.1017/9781009482578

© Azwihangwisi Edward Muthivhi 2026

This publication is in copyright. Subject to statutory exception and to the provisions of relevant collective licensing agreements, with the exception of the Creative Commons version the link for which is provided below, no reproduction of any part may take place without the written permission of Cambridge University Press & Assessment.

An online version of this work is published at doi.org/10.1017/9781009482578 under a Creative Commons Open Access license CC-BY-NC 4.0 which permits re-use, distribution and reproduction in any medium for non-commercial purposes providing appropriate credit to the original work is given and any changes made are indicated. To view a copy of this license visit https://creativecommons.org/licenses/by-nc/4.0

When citing this work, please include a reference to the DOI 10.1017/9781009482578

First published 2026

A catalogue record for this publication is available from the British Library

ISBN 978-1-009-48256-1 Hardback
ISBN 978-1-009-48255-4 Paperback
ISSN 2755-1202 (online)
ISSN 2755-1199 (print)

Additional resources of the publication available at www.Cambridge.org/Muthivhi

Cambridge University Press & Assessment has no responsibility for the persistence or accuracy of URLs for external or third-party internet websites referred to in this publication and does not guarantee that any content on such websites is, or will remain, accurate or appropriate.

For EU product safety concerns, contact us at Calle de José Abascal, 56, 1°, 28003 Madrid, Spain, or email eugpsr@cambridge.org

Decolonizing Pedagogy in Post-Apartheid South Africa

A Post-Vygotskian Ethicopolitical and Ontoepistemic Postulation

Elements in Critical Issues in Teacher Education

DOI: 10.1017/9781009482578
First published online: January 2026

Azwihangwisi Edward Muthivhi
University of Pretoria
Author for correspondence: Azwihangwisi Edward Muthivhi,
Azwihangwisi.muthivhi@up.ac.za

Abstract: This Element examines post-apartheid pedagogy in South Africa to uncover philosophical and epistemological foundations on which it is predicated. The analysis reveals quaint epistemologies and their associated philosophical postulations, espousing solipsistic methodologies that position teachers and their students as passive participants in activities rendered abstract and contemplative – an intellectual odyssey and dispassionate pursuit of knowledge devoid of context and human subjectivity. To counteract the effects of such coercive epistemologies and Western orthodoxies, a decolonising approach, prioritising ethical grounding of knowledge and pedagogy, is proposed. In this decolonising approach to learning and development, students enact the knowledge they embody, and, through such enactment of their culturally situated knowledge practices, students perceive concepts in their process of transformation and, consequently, acquire knowledge as tools for critical engagement with reality – and tools for meaningful pursuit of self-knowledge, agency, and identity development. This title is also available as Open Access on Cambridge Core.

This Element also has a video abstract:
www.cambridge.org/EITE_Muthivhi_abstract

Keywords: decolonising pedagogy, transformative agency, post-apartheid pedagogy, Vygotsky, Stetsenko

© Azwihangwisi Edward Muthivhi 2026

ISBNs: 9781009482561 (HB), 9781009482554 (PB), 9781009482578 (OC)
ISSNs: 2755-1202 (online), 2755-1199 (print)

Contents

Introduction — 1

1 Political and Historical Foundations of Neoliberal Pedagogy — 4

2 Transformative Agency and Identity Development — 12

3 Ontoepistemic Grounding of Contemporary Post-Apartheid Pedagogy — 20

4 Connecting Pedagogy to Culturally Situated Community Practices and Knowledge Traditions — 34

5 Ethical and Political Grounding of Knowledge and Pedagogy — 63

References — 71

Introduction

The early to mid 1990s was a period of much hope for schooling in South Africa and society at large, brought about by the long anticipated sociopolitical transformation from apartheid to democratic order. For the first time, South African society was expected to normalise from the turmoil that had threatened to destroy it. In particular, the apartheid pedagogy, and the widespread failure that had characterised it, was expected to become a thing of the past. The new sociopolitical dispensation was expected to usher in new schooling underpinned by transformative and decolonised pedagogy that would overhaul and bring to an end the colonial and apartheid practices with their coercive and hierarchical consequences on society and schooling. As a result, robust debates about what form a viable post-apartheid pedagogy could look like had already resumed and, by the mid 1980s, approaches and models had already begun to be put forth for consideration.

For example, Miller (1984) proposed that pedagogy on the part of African students must enable them to engender Western culture and thought processes. In the same vein, Miller (1984) argued that models of schooling based on cultural relativism, such as the model proposed by Cole (1996) in regard to minority students in the United States of America would essentially reproduce the same inequalities which had resulted from the apartheid segregated schooling system. Consequently, Miller (1984) argued that such an approach to pedagogy for African students would inevitably lead to the promotion of what he called 'cultural zoos', which would effectively lock African students in their cultural milieus and thereby restrict their conceptual capacity for successful learning and development as had happened under the apartheid schooling (Matusov, 2008; Miller, 1984).

Consequently, Matusov (2008), in his review of this approach, argues that these South African authors, in their adherence to what he termed a universalist viewpoint that posits knowledge as universal and objective, and knowledge as devoid of human subjectivity, had assumed a hierarchical viewpoint that rank and file cultures and civilisations. According to this view, Western culture is viewed as leading the way and setting the standard of human historical development which manifests as knowledge practices and traditions of schooling, with African culture and other non-Western civilisations marching behind Western civilisation and its manifestation in Western logic and associated philosophical postulations – as the unfolding *telios* of culture and history.

Indeed, as with studies of pedagogy in other parts of the world (Cole, 1996) research had already established that African students approached knowledge and school learning differently from what was expected within Western schooling systems. For example, Van Vlaenderen (1999) reports that African students in her study demonstrated knowledge assumptions, concepts, and problem-solving that involved the perception of knowledge as 'situationally bound', emphasising 'reciprocal interdependence with others', and foregrounding 'social harmony'. At the same time, these students assumed inherent connectedness between 'cognitive and affective aspects' of knowledge (Van Vlaenderen, 1999, pp. 172–173). Van Vlaenderen (1999) concluded, therefore, that these young people – contrary to dominant assumptions within western schooling – perceived the process of solving problems as predominantly interpersonal. That is, according to Van Vlaenderen (1999), these African students perceived knowledge and truth as not absolute – not objective, and not independent of those who defined knowledge and truth.

As a result, Van Vlaenderen (1999) called for these students to be assisted to relinquish these culturally constrained ways of thinking and problem solving and, instead, be provided with more efficient cultural tools for competing on the global stage. Consequently, Van Vlaenderen (1999) proposes that African students need to be exposed to knowledge within western traditions of schooling so as to enable them to relinquish their constrained, culturally derived conceptual approaches to knowledge and problem solving and adopt more powerful and effective approaches to learning and concept development, possible only through Western forms of schooling and knowledge practices.

Further, in response to recent calls by student movements such as #Rhodesmustfall and #Feesmustfall, as well as the related groups in South Africa and beyond, a number of critical commentaries on the subject of decolonisation have emerged. For example, Jansen (2019) dismisses calls for decolonisation on grounds that such decolonisation would be akin to what he calls retrogressive 'nativism' and a 'retreat to indigenization' (Jansen, 2017, p. 167; 2019, p. 62). At the same time, calls for decolonisation of pedagogy were dismissed on grounds that the proposed decolonisation approach resembled 'narrow', 'essentialist', and 'isolatory practices', contrary to 'genuine decolonization' agenda (Griffiths, 2019, p. 6).

Further, and ironically, decolonisation of pedagogy was also dismissed on grounds that it would be tantamount to relativism. According to Griffiths (2019), in agreement with Mbebe (2016), genuine decolonisation requires 'an active reckoning with the forces of globalization'. Consequently, South Africa's poor Black majority are called upon to reckon with the 'forces of globalization' that require 'the acceptance of the Humboldtian University in the global South' (Griffiths, 2019, p. 6). However, the irony of the Humboldtian ideal herein proposed is that the idea embodies the very essence of self-constrained individualism, including the associated contemplative postulations that the decolonising approaches, in fact, seek to challenge and overcome.

One of the only sympathetic approaches to calls for decolonising pedagogy emanating from contemporary scholarship in South Africa, perhaps, comes from scholars working in areas related to the Vygotskian framework such as Joanne Hardman. Hardman argues 'for a pedagogy that includes the voice of the previously marginalised in a pedagogical developmental space in which a culturally more competent other (the teacher) guides the student towards the co-construction of meaning as a mechanism for decolonial pedagogy'. However, Hardman thinks that such an approach fails 'because pedagogy is political' and one 'requires enormous political will to shift the structures that have existed for centuries (Hardman (2024, p.156)). According to Hardman, therefore, such a change can be difficult because it may be experienced as epistemic violence directed on established ways of knowing. Therefore, Hardman (2024) proposes 'a Kierkegaardian leap of faith' involving 'critical engagement with the colonial canon and its pedagogical basis', re-evaluating how teachers teach and prioritising 'the kind of knowledge that students need to navigate the 21st century' (Hardman, 2024, p. 156).

To expand, from the present approach to decolonising pedagogy, I would propose that it is the contemporary post-apartheid pedagogy and its associated Western canons that render epistemic violence to students, eroding their agency and creativity and positioning them as passively adapting to the objective meanings of the fixed curriculum products within contemporary, post-apartheid pedagogy. Therefore, in applying the concept of praxis, grounded on the work of Vygotsky, Freire, and Hedegaard as Hardman (2024) proposes, I would agree with the proposition to critically engage the colonial canon, but such engagement needs to be premised on *praxis*, simultaneously committing to the transformation of the contemporary post-apartheid pedagogy and its underlying coersive epistemologies. That is, rather than prioritising only the epistemic and the rational at the expense of the moral and the ethical, and thereby denying culturally situated community practices and the associated knowledge traditions, decolonising pedagogy approach should ground teaching and learning on students' personal interests, goals, and emotions.

Therefore, as a personal attempt at contributing towards a solution regarding the problem of colonial pedagogy and its dismissal of non-Western, culturally situated approaches, this book therefore analyses the prevailing post-apartheid pedagogy in South Africa to reveal its inherent limitations, thereby proposing a model premised on a contradictory moral vision that potentially offer a viable alternative to the prevailing conditions. Inspired by the recent groundbreaking work of Stetsenko (2023, 2021, 2020a, 2019b), the book offers a personal quest for knowledge, and a personal struggle for self-realization and agentive contribution to our rapidly changing, yet still precarious, post-apartheid society with its schooling and pedagogy that have, unfortunately, failed to live up to the expectations. This, indeed, is simultaneously a moral–ethical quest to contribute towards the debunking of 'stifling cannons and prescriptions of the hegemonic ... entailments' of eurocentric epistemologies that underpin contemporary post-apartheid pedagogy in South Africa, and thereby move beyond its prescriptions of 'confining parameters of what qualifies as knowledge' (Stetsenko, 2023, p. 18).

The book, therefore, achieves this goal by positing an ethico-political grounding of pedagogy. That is, the contemporary post-apartheid pedagogy, and its epistemic grounding of knowledge, is superseded by the ethical grounding of the values of equity and social justice. Therefore, the epistemic grounding of knowledge is subsumed under higher-order categories, and the ethical grounding, to do–not only with questions of truth and rationality, but subsuming these under ethical dimension of knowledge to do with what, under prevailing historical and political conditions, 'should', or 'ought' to be the principles underpinning pedagogy and its organisation.

Therefore, the book demonstrates how pedagogy and knowldge grounded on epistemic criteria – as is generally the case with contemporary post-apartheid pedagogy – could translate into coercive practices that stifle possibilities for transformative pedagogy, while at the same serving to prop the very structures that reproduce inequalities in society and schooling.

1 Political and Historical Foundations of Neoliberal Pedagogy

> *Pedagogics is never and was never politically indifferent, since, willingly or unwillingly, through its own work on the psyche, it has always adopted a particular social pattern, political line, in accordance with the dominant social class that has guided its interests.*
>
> (Vygotsky, 1997, p. 348)

1.1 Introduction

Schooling in South Africa has a long history, beginning with the traditional schools which were part of the pre-colonial sociopolitical context. This schooling, well-established and spanning centuries, reflected the prevailing social system and life experiences of pre-colonial societies. However, pre-colonial schooling has received little attention through the colonial and apartheid regimes in South Africa, and their legitimacy has often been questioned from the beginning, going back to missionary schooling as precursor to colonial education (Muthivhi, 2010).

Western colonial advance in Southern Africa began with the Portuguese navigation around the Cape of Good Hope in the fifteenth century, paving the way for the first colonial settlement to be established by the Dutch at the foot of Table Mountain a century and a half later in 1652. Enslin and Hedge (2023) argue that colonialism, generally, was responsible for much looting of resources from the colonised countries for the building of Western imperial powers. In their wording:

> Alongside the plundering of colonies' wealth, this era saw the imposition of imperial military and administrative power, dispossession of indigenous people's land, impoverishment, acts of genocide, famine, exploitation of labour including through slavery and indentured labour, and the enforcement of trade on terms that favoured and enriched the colonial powers. A key feature of the colonial era, with radical implications for education, was dismissal of both local custom and the capabilities of colonized people, in a racist social order. (Enslin and Hedge, 2023, p. 3)

The colonial system, therefore, was inextricably interwoven with the expansion of Western trade, extraction of natural resources, and slavery mainly to provide labour for the plantation industry, especially in the so-called new world. There has, therefore, been an indelible relationship between Western colonial expansion and political and economic activity from the beginning.

While colonialism in the traditional form in which Western colonial powers occupied and controlled the colonised nations was gradually relinquished by the mid twentieth century in Africa, the extractive and exploitative practices associated with the system, as Enslin and Hedge (2023) argue, did not end. On the contrary, the practices continued under the neocolonial and neo-empiricist guise, in the form of neoliberal capitalism, with new imperial powers such as post-Soviet Russia and China, alongside the United States, assuming dominant position during the twentieth century. Consequently, as Enslin and Hedge (2023) argue, the advance to free-market capitalism would probably not have been achieved in Europe had it not been for the prior successes of colonial expansions.

Contemporary global colonial expansion therefore fostered the creation of what Enslin and Hedge (2023) term 'new forms of less tangible Empire', propelled by 'global circuits of production', linked to global capitalist market economy (Enslin and Hedge, 2023, p. 7). There is evidently a deeply entrenched interconnection between colonial expansion and the goals of political economy – namely, labour exploitation and resource extraction. Such a predatory and expansionist economic activity undoubtedly eschewed responsibility and accountability obligations associated with regulatory sociopolitical structures.

As Enslin and Hedge (2023) argue, the sociopolitical and economic expansionist activities of Western colonial regimes were inevitably institutionalised, with education coming to serve as the instrument of legitimation and validation of the evolving system. That is, schooling, and knowledge in general, was subjected to the evolving logic of colonialism. As a result, knowledge – and education – served to justify and legitimise the logic of the evolving world order and its inherent injustices. At the same time, the validity of indigenous culture, knowledge practices and traditions, was systematically undermined. Concomitantly, colonial structures and their associated extractive and exploitative practices were rendered logical consequences of historical development and nature-given biological inevitabilities. Indeed, this line of research and its egregious and shameful claims continue into the present day. Its implications are felt, especially in such baseless claims suggesting that the oppressed and disadvantaged populations – both in formerly colonised societies and within former colonial nations – are innately inferior and in fact deserving of their social status. Such research agendas, unfortunately, follow on the heels of recent proliferation of research that continues to emphasise biological reductionism and genetic determinism, including claims about rankable intelligence (Stetsenko, 2023). In post-apartheid South Africa's neocolonial scholarship, such supremacist ideas are not uncommon. In their unmistaken and most obtrusive form, such behaviour was blatantly displayed in the recent research by Nieuwoudt et al. (2019), who claim that women of colour, or so-called Coloured[1] women, have inferior cognitive abilities compared to their white counterparts.

Consequently, according to Enslin and Hedge (2023), contemporary neoliberal research agenda – realised through its associated neocolonial practices – is experienced in the resurgence of global standardised testing, global ranking of schooling and universities, as well as in global benchmarking practices, including the postulation of norms and performance standards on criteria that favour Western powers. At the same time, ambiguous concepts and skewed notions about standards are produced with the effect of reproducing the injustices, as well as the inequalities that have characterised colonial relations of domination and control (Enslin and Hedge, 2023).

In a similar vein, Young (2007) provides an outline of the British neoliberal ideology, arguing that contemporary schooling and pedagogy in the United Kingdom of Great Britain (UK) have evolved from neoliberal free-market capitalism. According to Young (2007), neoliberals believed in market deregulation, namely, that the government should refrain from regulating markets. In their view, the government must cease regulating markets as this would have

---

[1] The term 'Coloured' was coined by the apartheid regime to refer to people of mixed European and African descent, including the indigenous Khoi-San communities and the descendants of the Cape Malay or Muslim communities who came from Southeast Asia during the nineteenth-century European slave trade network. Although the term is still in circulation, even in official government policies, it is nonetheless not accepted by everyone in these communities as a form of polite referential.

a positive impact on reducing government spending. As a consequence of neoliberal policies, according to Young (2007), schools in the UK came to be organised along the lines of free-market capitalism, with greater emphasis on aspects such as outcomes, results, and standardised assessment. At the same time, schools were defined in instrumental terms – 'as a means to an end', and 'a delivery agency' that is geared for the 'needs of the economy'. Schools were also defined as a form of a 'quasi-market' for 'mass vocationalism' (Young, 2007, p. 12).

According to Young (2007), education came to serve the economic goal of securing employment and for participation in a free-market capitalist economy. Therefore, pedagogy in post-industrial UK came to be defined in terms of 'products' or 'outcomes' – as opposed to 'process' and 'quality engagement'. The consequence was inevitable: schools came to be 'driven by targets, assignments and league tables', with students becoming disinterested and their teachers experiencing burnout (Young, 2007, p. 12). Therefore, schooling organised along the line of neoliberal thinking came to be envisioned in instrumental terms, as a quasi-market environment with commodified knowledge – with knowledge, its *de facto* product – contrived in terms of market value proposition. In this rendering of knowledge and pedagogy, the value of schooling was taken to reside in the market value of its products, outcomes, and concepts.

1.2 Pedagogy as Market Commodity

Neoliberal values therefore favoured commodification and marketisation of knowledge and pedagogy, as well as subjecting the processes of teaching and learning – including the associated procedures for assessing learning performance – and the success of the teaching strategies and related methodologies, to the vagaries of market economy. As Young (2007) has argued, pedagogy, the process of teaching and learning, is rendered instrumental to the goals of market products and value proposition of commodities. As a result, the quality of human subjective engagements is superseded by the technology of producing outcomes – meaningless products and mechanical activities cast in the ideology of adapting to, fitting in, and coping with the demands of fixed curriculum products.

Consequently, neoliberal model of pedagogy, and its neocolonial predicate, artificially disentangles the knowledge production process from its inherent human subjectivity, emotions, values, motives, goals, and interests. The process inevitably dehumanises sociocultural practices and renders classroom activities meaningless and mechanistic. This situation undoubtedly has far-reaching consequences when revealed from the unique and specific sociocultural context of African classrooms where students are often subjected to learning not only in a language they have scarcely mastered but from within the epistemological point of view and approaches to knowledge far removed from their specific culturally situated worldview postulation.

Loughland and Sriprakash (2016), for example, have demonstrated how the neoliberal approach within the Australian context has failed minority students, while its associated capitalist market economic system ensured that the envisaged reforms continue to benefit the privileged class, despite the original intention of reforming the system in favour of indigenous minorities. That is, according to Loughland and Sriprakash (2016), the neoliberal political discourse of 'equity and excellence' deflected attention away from the real conditions of systemic structural inequities within schooling and society. Therefore, by reconstituting the discourse of equity and quality/excellence and transmuting it into 'market enhancing mechanisms' that benefit middle-class interests and neoliberal values of 'individual positional advantage', knowledge and pedagogy were rendered commodified products. Knowledge was, consequently, evaluated based on its perceived market value, where acquisition became 'dependent upon the wealth and wishes of parents, rather than the ability and efforts of pupils' (Loughland and Sriprakash, 2016, p. 243).

1.3 No Child Left Behind

The concept of school knowledge, and pedagogy, as commodified products whose value is dependent on the vagaries of the markets and therefore benefiting advantaged social classes which, in contemporary neocolonial societies, is increasingly racialised, has been discussed in the work of Matusov (2011). In addressing the consequences of pedagogy premised on the neoliberal capitalist agenda vis-à-vis efficacy, well-being, and equity of teachers and students, Matusov (2011) discusses the contradictory nature of the neoliberal ideology informing the *No Child Left Behind* policy. Matusov (2011) argues that the philosophical premises of the neoliberal political system in the United States, comprising the belief in self-constrained individual, competition, accountability, and meritocracy, as well as the associated notions of quality and standards, actually work against the learning and educational progress ideals that underpin the *No Child Left Behind* policy.

Consequently, Matusov (2011) proposes a form of schooling and pedagogy that is not only oriented towards the acquisition and mastery of the formal discipline and skills, including literacy acquisition and the teaching and learning of reading and writing. Therefore, for Matusov (2011), moving beyond these traditional neoliberal postulations should comprise what he terms 'socially and personally valuable practices and activities' (Matusov, 2011, p. 6).

With regard to literacy instruction, the approach prioritising students' socially and personally valuable practices and activities would involve gaining access to literacy for *self-mastery* and *social contribution*, as opposed to merely mastering the formal discipline or subject matter knowledge. That is, the self-directed teaching and learning activities within the proposed approach would be directed not only by teachers but, and importantly, by the students. This approach, therefore, connects classroom activities to 'participation in games, participation in search for information, leisure, social activism, and participation in arts, including many other activities requiring literacy' (Matusov, 2011, p. 6).

Matusov's (2011) approach has important implications for the proposed decolonising approach, favouring authentic connection of pedagogy to students' valuable social and personal practices geared at social contribution and self-mastery. The practices valuable to students and situated in their own society and culture would comprise games, artistic activities such as musical heritage, dramatic events, and related sociopolitical and linguistic practices. For a decolonising approach to pedagogy, nonetheless, the practices of society and culture valuable and significant to students in their personal pursuit of knowledge and self-realisation are not connected by way of merely adding to pre-existing neoliberal practices.

Therefore, it is not a matter of accommodating one to the either for the sake of appearing progressive, tolerant, and accommodating, in the usual manner in which neoliberal ideology often pacifies calls for social justice and equality. Incompatible aspects of pre-existing practices are negated at the same time as the ones that turn out to be potentially compatible are continued in new ways, in the sense of them being subsumed into new forms of learning-being-doing (Stetsenko, 2007). Therefore, predicating the decolonising approach on ethical grounding and emphasising the practical, real-world everyday experiences of students and their agentic contribution to social transformation, self-development, and identity inevitably render the process emancipatory. That is, the decolonising approach to pedagogy must be geared towards the ethical-political imperative of social justice and equity, especially given the prevailing political and historical conditions of post-apartheid schooling and society.

1.4 Loss of Agency and Alienation

The negative consequences of neoliberal reforms of schooling in the Netherlands were explored by van Oers (2015), in specific regard to the loss of agency on the part of teachers and their students. van Oers reports of the experiences of alienation that results from the conflict between formal, prescribed knowledge and concepts' meanings, on the one hand, and teachers' and students' personal sense, on the other hand. The loss of personal motive and will is brought about by the demands for teachers and students to follow strict requirements, including formal procedures and methodologies that conflict with their capacity for agentic contribution and personal motives.

That is, consequent to the reforms aimed at bridging the gap between preschool four- to five-year-old students, on the one hand, and primary school six- to seven-year-olds, on the other hand, by requiring that preschool pedagogy includes more 'programme-centred' and 'direct teaching' activities emphasising learning to read, learning to write, and doing arithmetic on the other hand. Further, primary school children were required to include the pedagogy of the preschool children, involving giving more time for students to participate in play, as well as participating in activities that promote the development of basic social skills and good conduct. These changes resulted in many teachers on both sides of the spectrum experiencing 'conflicting motives'. That is, the teachers experienced the new approaches as limiting their choice and consequently, eroding their agency. According to van Oers (2015), therefore, this fixed curriculum, premised on the idea of 'school as an economic production factor', renders teachers and their students passive, and weakens students' ability to make sense of a problem situation by relating it to personal motives, interests, and values (van Oers, 2015).

At the same time, according to van Oers (2015), curriculum contents and structures are revealed as neutral instruments which can be implemented in mechanical ways, a situation which undermines the goals of fostering agency, critical reflection, innovation, creativity, and social responsibility. At the same time, concepts, skills and values become commodified, taking up objectified meanings subject to dispassionate pursuit, as well as the associated solipsistic and contemplative methodologies. The consequence of such objectification of meanings undoubtedly leads to alienation, and the consequent loss of agency and identity development. Therefore, van Oers (2015) proposes a *play-based pedagogy* for reinforcing agency on the part of teachers and students. According to this approach 'playfully formatted activities' become the 'auxiliary means' or mediating tools for overcoming the unwarranted assumption that pedagogy can be implemented with teachers merely serving the role of mechanically linking subject matter knowledge and concepts to students' subjective experiences (van Oers, 2015, p. 20). Consequently, van Oers (2015) argues that the model assisted teachers to act with agency, and to be creative and innovative in their teaching, meaningfully connecting pedagogy to the needs and interests of their students while simultaneously achieving the political demands of objectified meanings for the transmission of culture and heritage.

1.5 Conclusion

There undoubtedly is a long political and historical association between contemporary schooling and pedagogy within Western colonial powers and their former colonised nations, and this association is, at the same time, indelibly intertwined with the neoliberal philosophy, which combines the goals of the free market economy with that of modern schooling and pedagogy. In the free market economic goals, the vagaries of the market hold sway on schooling and the goals of pedagogy, and, as a result, knowledge, concepts, and methodologies are rendered absolute, while the activities of teaching and learning are reduced to fitting in and coping with objectified meanings and pre-established models.

Such pedagogy, organised around the goals of free market economic system, proffering values of competition, solipsism, and standardisation, unfortunately transmutes school knowledge, and pedagogy, into commodified products defined in terms of economic goals of meeting the needs of employment and economic growth. Consequently, outcomes, targets, and league tables – that is, the results and products, as opposed to process and quality teaching and learning become standard criteria for evaluating performance goals. The process is akin to what has been termed the 'regime and ideology of adaptation [that] position and prescribe people to be powerless, mindless, and isolated, like mechanical cogs in the wheels of capitalist production' (Stetsenko, 2023, p. 23).

Such is the inevitable consequence of what Loughland and Sriprakash (2016), citing Apple (2001), have termed 'the sinister acts of the invisible hand of the market' (Loughland and Sriprakash, 2016, p. 246). The tragedy of this hegemonic and coercive view of knowledge and pedagogy that prescribes knowledge as absolute and neutral, is that it dehumanises teachers and their students, while disempowering and alienating their interactivities and practices. At the same time, members of community, including their community practices, are viewed as having no authority and making no difference to what goes on within schooling, the process of knowledge production and its dissemination, including its enactment as classroom and school pedagogy.

In its erroneous assumption that curriculum – its contents and structures – constitutes a neutral instrument which can be implemented in mechanical ways, neoliberal approach to pedagogy undermines the goals of fostering agency, critical reflection, innovation, creativity, and social responsibility. At the same time, knowledge and its products such as concepts, skills, and values become commodified, subject to dispassionate pursuit of mindless, solipsistic, and contemplative activities which naturally produce objectification and, consequently, alienation and loss of agency. Such a condition evidently becomes even more pronounced and debilitating when it comes to students and their teachers subjected to colonial and neoliberal pedagogy that denies their reality of injustices and inequalities, thereby usurping their legitimate role and place, hence, agentic contribution to social transformation and self-development.

2 Transformative Agency and Identity Development

2.1 Introduction

In contradistinction to the political ideology of adaptation, premised on ethos of fitting in and conforming with the status quo of what is already in place and taken for granted – to borrow from Stetsenko's (2023) postulation, as comprising the overarching adaptationist ethos prevalent in eurocentric models of knowledge and pedagogy – the transformative worldview postulated in the current approach to decolonising pedagogy prioritises creativity and innovation, realised as social contribution at the intersection of individual and collective agency. From this particular approach, dubbed Transformative Activist Stance (TAS) (Stetsenko, 2020b), human development—consciousness, human nature, is viewed as grounded, purposeful, and answerable. That is, social practices realise social life and social reality, while such practices are – simultaneously, realised through people contributing to social transformation at the intersection of individual and collective agency, with particular emphasis on the sought-after future.

Therefore, contrary to the ethos of acquiescing to the status quo of coercive Western ethnocentric epistemologies that prioritise passive adaptation to pre-established canons and prescribed methodologies, the transformative worldview for decolonising pedagogy posits an ontology grounded on agentic contribution to social transformation, simultaneously premised on a bidirectional nexus, and an ineluctable unity, of individual and collective practices. Indeed, such practices emerge as always future-oriented while simultaneously embodied by, situated in, as well as grounded on historical practices of society and culture which are enacted through answerable deeds in the here-and-now of individual-collective activity. Consequently, the individual is viewed as fully and indelibly subsumed in the collective, while simultaneously contributing, agentively, to collective social transformation and self-realisation.

This rendering of a non-dualistic ontology to decolonising pedagogy has important implications. Among these implications are the overcoming of a dualist postulation of Cartesian epistemologies and their associated hierarchical and hegemonic methodologies that are conducive for racism, injustices, and inequalities. At the same time, the transformative worldview herein proposed transcends the mutually exclusive and contradictory postulations of objectivist ontology, on the one hand, and the thoroughgoing collectivist methodologies of the sociocultural approaches and many traditional models of decolonisation epistemologies, on the other hand. At the core of these contradictory and relativist approaches advancing self-serving forms of ethnocentrism and hence insisting on exclusionary models of knowledge and pedagogy, are models that prescribe pernicious individualism and solipsism, on the one hand, and those that advance thoroughgoing collectivism, on the other – reducing personhood and individual contribution to collective social processes and practices. As a result, unique individual contribution is submerged within collective social practices, with the implication, as Stetsenko (2023) has argued, that 'the person cannot find her due – and non-individualistic place – within accounts of social processes and practices' (Stetsenko, 2023, p. 23).

2.2 Transformative Agency and Identity Development

The current approach to decolonising pedagogy conceptualises agency as premised on the notion of agentic contribution to collective communal practices, as an ontological foundation of human development, human being, and the actual process of becoming human. This standpoint is simultaneously inspired by the age-old African *ubuntu ontology*, which postulates the profound and ineluctable unity of humans, including non-human species. According to this postulation, humans bring about and realise their humanity through their affirmation of the humanity of other human beings, both living and past – including their non-human natural world. The emphasis is therefore on future-oriented action of mutual affirmation as the ontological foundation of being human, and therefore humanity itself is posited as a *process* that essentially rests on answerable deeds, oriented towards each other with the goal of creating and sustaining a viable future (Foster, 2010; Tutu, 2005).

The emphasis on interdependence and social harmony as a process that human beings create and through which they come into being resonates with contemporary developments in cultural-historical activity frameworks. For example, Engeström et al. (2014) explain that transformative agency differs from conventional notions of agency because, rather than espousing mere individual action, transformative agency involves action derived from and simultaneously oriented towards social transformation. The authors further contend that transformative agency stems from encounters with 'conflicts' and 'contradictions' in collective activity, emerging from and evolving over prolonged periods of time. Therefore, transformative agency goes beyond the 'situational here-and-now, developing participants' joint activity by explicating and envisioning new possibilities for collective change efforts' (Engeström et al., 2014, p. 124).

By establishing the indelible connections of individuals and community practices and society, the concept of transformative agency overcomes traditional dichotomies that characterised agency as exclusively associated with individuals, and the social as thoroughly collective and devoid of individual contribution. In this conceptualisation of agency, the ontological primacy is premised on collaborative social practices as involving people acting and doing things together, while simultaneously creating their life through answerable deeds, life quests, and meaningful pursuits enacted as collective efforts and struggles for a sought after future (Stetsenko, 2020a). Therefore, in superseding the dualistic epistemologies of isolated individuals that deny human creativity and innovation, on the one hand, and the wholesale collectivist approaches that deny a place and role for individual contribution, on the other hand, the current, decolonising approach focuses on agentic contributions as a new form of life, and an ontological primacy of answerable deeds that connect humans with each other into an unavoidable and profound interconnectedness that constitutes the deepest and most important feature of all human life (Stetsenko, 2020a; 2007).

This view of human nature, being, and human development, as grounded in answerable deeds of collective social practices, and as the matrix through which agency is enacted, has important implications for schooling and classroom pedagogy. In postulating a view of pedagogy and identity development, Vianna and Stetsenko (2011) argue for a perspective that links the processes situated in communal practices to students' 'forward-looking' and activist practices of social transformation. This connection of pedagogy to agentic contribution is made possible by students' own active recreation of cultural tools, vis-à-vis their potential application in future practices 'as tools of meaningful quest and, therefore, identity' (Vianna and Stetsenko, 2011, p. 320).

Identity development, therefore, is not taken to be merely an outcome of teaching and learning, but the very substance and fabric of pedagogy, as well as the vehicle through which pedagogy is realised. According to this view, knowledge is transformed – both by teachers and their students – into tools for social transformation of self-realisation, as well as a tool for meaningful pursuit of self-knowledge and hence, identity development (Vianna and Stetsenko, 2011). Therefore, according to this view, a pedagogy grounded on ethos of agentive contribution to social transformation and identity development demands that teachers and their students take charge of the process of classroom teaching and learning and assume a moral position vis-à-vis knowledge and its associated ontological assumptions, thereby transforming knowledge through an active recreation of cultural tools, as an enactment of the envisioned future and identity development.

According to this view, teaching is organised in ways where knowledge is revealed as deriving from social practice and carried out through cultural tools such as language, concepts, models, and various symbolic means – including the embodied culturally situated community practices and knowledge traditions. Consequently, knowledge is recreated by students through their active and agentive exploration and inquiry and, consequently, rendered meaningful in the light of its relevance to students' significant activities (Vianna and Stetsenko, 2011).

Therefore, as opposed to neoliberal notions of identity that prioritises isolation and self-interested solipsism, including alienation, identity development in the transformative worldview herein proposed prioritises profound human interconnectedness, collective collaborative practices, togetherness, care for others, and communal solidarity. The notion of identity development is therefore severed from the dichotomous assumptions and the associated entailments of difference, separation, and opposition, such as in the postulation of racial segregation and tribal-ethnic ideologies that underpinned the colonial and apartheid regimes. Identity development in the transformative worldview postulation, grounded on values of solidarity, care, and responsibility, emphasises the positive ethos of common good, justice, and equity. There is therefore no room for the negative implications of segregation and division along racial, ethnic, gender, religious, and the various incarnations that make up the root cause of many of today's tragic consequences of divisions and disharmony.

2.3 Ethos of Agentic Contribution to Collective Community Practices

An approach to pedagogy narrowly grounded on epistemic questions, completely impervious to issues to do with moral visions, as well as the related issues of justice and equity, is inevitably destined to fail, as has happened with the contemporary post-apartheid pedagogy in South Africa. A decolonising pedagogy approach premised on ethos of agentive contribution to collective community practices, social transformation, and self-realisation prioritises the philosophical centrality of activism. As a result, the ethos of adaptation, participation, and political quietism, associated with Western dualist epistemologies, are superseded by an approach to knowledge that places human development, reality, and human nature at the nexus of social practices. At the same time, such agentive contributions to social practices, grounded in purposeful and answerable deeds at the intersection of individual and collective agency, places particular emphasis on the sought-after future.

There is therefore a convergence of ethical, political, ontological, as well as the epistemological into an ethico-onto epistemological grounding of subjectivity. As Stetsenko (2019b) elaborates, all acts, knowing, and pedagogy presuppose a forward-looking activism. This is the activism that implies a forward-looking, purposive action of changing the world in view of a sought-after future. Therefore, human subjectivity, in its entailment of the goals of agentive contribution to collective communal practices, social transformation, and self-realisation, is both future-oriented and inherently ethical. That is, as Stetsenko (2019a) argues, it is impossible to imagine a future without locating ourselves in its present and history, while, at the same time, we cannot situate ourselves in the present and its history unless we are able to imagine its future and, simultaneously, commit to create or bring that future about.

Therefore, knowledge becomes possible within the frame of these commitments and identifications of possible futures. The ethical dimension regarding what is good and what is bad, what is right and what is wrong, including decisions about what to do next, framed within the imagined goals of a sought after future, grounds all action possibilities. Consequently, projected future-oriented goals, as imagined endpoints, define the whole dynamic process of human development as an agentic contribution to collective social practices. It is this inherent human subjectivity which arises as an activist process of committing to a sought-after future that, according the Stetsenko (2019a),

> ... position us to see *what is* through the prism of *how* the present situations and conditions *came to be* and, also, in light of the imagined and sought-after future – of what we believe *ought to be*. Thus, the historicity and situativity of knowledge are ascertained alongside the focus on its ineluctable fusion with an activist future-oriented stance. An endpoint defines the whole dynamics of human development and society, of knowing-being-doing; without and endpoint (albeit flexible and ever-changing, like a horizon that shifts with every step we make), it is impossible to move forward, to move at all. (Stetsenko, 2019a, p. 9, emphasis in original)

2.4 Knowledge as a 'Whole Process of Inquiry'

The process of knowledge production – that is, knowing the world and self, rendered into an agentic contribution to social transformation and self-realisation – is therefore posited as always grounded and purposeful. The world is therefore knowable only within, and through, a process of bringing it about, as a process not separate from humans who contribute to the process of its production. That is, the world is not viewed as separate, isolated, and devoid of meaning and subjectivity, as made up of disenchanted matter only knowable through objective, value free pursuit of disinterested facts about, and models of, reality.

Therefore, knowledge from the transformative perspective herein postulated, is taken to be akin to Thelen's (2005) metaphor of human development: a ceaseless mountain stream, moving all the time in a dynamic flow of ceaseless changes and continuities. As Stetsenko (2023) elaborates, like a ceaseless mountain stream, knowledge production can as well be viewed as a dynamic process embodying the past history in the present while carrying it into the future. Like a stream with no predetermined structure, knowledge production process is non-linear, with no rigid prediction of next stages and end goals, embodying the past in the present, out of which future possibilities are curved. Likewise, knowledge production needs to be understood as a whole dynamic system with mutually co-embedded, interdependent, intertwined, and mutually implicating elements. Like a stream, the process of knowledge production is posited to be fluid and continuous, with uninterrupted currents, eddies, milestones, contours, and plateaus. Therefore, knowledge can only be regarded as relatively reliable, comparatively predictive, almost warranted, and nearly certain but, if only, momentarily (Stetsenko, 2023).

There is therefore no room for absolute certainty, and a world posited as separate from human subjectivity and devoid of meaning – to be known *as it is*, once and for all. On the contrary, the process of knowledge production is posited as profoundly agentic, contextually situated, historically contingent, and practically relevant. The process, rather than proceeding as abstract, solipsistic, and mentalist endeavour, instead takes into account contextual relevance, cultural contingency, and personal needs, desires, and emotions.

As Stetsenko (2023), following John Dewey, has stated, knowledge cannot be taken to exist outside of inquiry. That is, inquiry is taken as the very process by which knowledge comes to exist. Outside of inquiry, knowledge becomes impossible. According to this view, the pursuit of knowledge is premised on asking questions and searching for answers, and knowledge is understood as a process of asking authentic questions and pursuing meaningful answers that matter for one's life conditions and lived reality. That is, knowledge is taken to be open-ended, indeterminate, as well as culturally situated, historically contingent, and practically relevant. Even more importantly, knowledge is taken to be politically non-neutral, such that knowledge production, and science, is understood to be inherently social, as well as politically and ideologically saturated, including culturally and historically contingent and, ultimately, ethically responsible. Therefore, as contextually embedded and culturally situated, as well as historically contingent, the process of knowledge production simultaneously reveals particular historical-political struggles taking place in society and is therefore far from being a neutral, uncommitted, and apolitical and ahistorical affair (Stetsenko, 2021).

Knowledge production, according to this point of view, has to incorporate all the various steps that make up the process of its production, taken as one fluid and dynamic whole, proceeding from actual life worlds, everyday-life circumstances and real-life conditions – actual doings and concrete actions, ethical deeds always cognisant of others – termed 'answerable deeds', taken as the axiological centre of our 'becoming-through-doing' (Bakhtin, 1993), cited in Stetsenko (2007, p. 754). Stetsenko captures this view of being and 'becoming-through-doing' as

> [a] process-like, continuous (uninterrupted) and dynamic (ever-changing and cumulative) unfolding and active pressing forward with one's life, as a stepping forward through deeds, as a becoming-through-doing ... captures the unitary character of this process as one seamless, continuous flow understandable only in its totality, as not reducible to a chain of single discrete episodes. (Stetsenko, 2007, p. 754)

This conceptualisation of human development as grounded on answerable deeds unfolding in collective practices and giving form to the totality of life resonates with the ubuntu ontology on the ethical grounding of human development through responsible deeds that affirm the humanity of others, as pathway to self-affirmation and, hence, becoming human. That is, the self, and being-human, is a process that obtains within and through a process involving ethical conduct towards other humans, thereby becoming more human. This process is intimately and profoundly connected to selfhood and knowledge production, as knowing-, or becoming-through-doing. The process inevitably leads to a mutual embedding and, simultaneously, an embodiment of collective social practices, including processes in nature, into an ineluctable unitary process of which Stetsenko has termed, 'a whole process of inquiry'. That is,

> Knowledge is made up of an inquiry process and as such, is itself an open-ended, never-ending process that can never be said to ever reach anything like a final destination, firm conclusion, full and certain, universal, valid once and for all, answer. There is nothing static or and no part of it – such as facts, notions, concepts, and ideas – can ever be universalized, reified (frozen in time), essentialized, or taken for granted by assuming their independent status outside of the ongoing and never-ending process of knowledge production (inquiry), with no finality and no absolute certainty at any point. (Stetsenko, 2023, p. 27)

2.5 Conclusion

The process of knowledge production – that is, knowing the world and self – is rendered non-dualistic, non-mentalist, and therefore unitary process grounded on the ontology of human fundamental interconnectedness which is non-additive, but arising out of our essential condition of being together – namely, togetherness, oneness, unity, solidarity, and communality. That is, as elaborated in the *ubuntu* ontology, human beings essentially attain their humanity and, hence, become human as a result of their own actions oriented towards other humans, caring for the others, taking responsibility of the others, and affirming the humanity of others. All these practical actions grounded on ethics of being human are realised in the context of humans-Being-with-each-other and carrying out actions that demonstrate their moral responsibility for other humans, as a precondition of, and a fulcrum for, Being-human and attaining humanity for self through the humanity of others. This is a unitary and therefore non-solipsistic approach, which re-establishes fundamental human connections as an ineluctable unitary process.

Therefore, the values of equity, social justice, and solidarity as grounding principles for human consciousness become the ontological foundation of agentic contribution to collective communal practices. Agency is therefore conceptualised as a condition of Being-human from the beginning, rooted in ethos of collective responsibility and contribution to collective practices. That is, agency is understood as unfolding through the process of imagining the future, as implicating the positioning of self in the evolving history of human-becoming. Therefore, agency emerges in, and through, the matrix of collective social practices – a form of human subjectivity that is politically and ideologically embedded, historically contingent, and culturally situated.

Contemporary post-apartheid pedagogy – including its knowledge postulation – unfortunately focuses only, and exclusively, on questions of epistemology, rationality, and the truth value of knowledge, at the expense of ethical dimension, involving questions of solidarity, equity and social justice. This negation of the historical and political struggles, and the associated moral commitment to particular horizons of possibility in the design of contemporary post-apartheid pedagogy, has unfortunately produced the prevailing alienation and loss of agency, widespread as the general outcome of schooling in post-apartheid South Africa. The next section provides a critical exposition of the epistemic grounding of knowledge and pedagogy, rendering knowledge universal and neutral and, hence, devoid of context and history. This analysis therefore debunks the myths of the 'ideology of no ideology' that posits knowledge, and pedagogy, as devoid of historical context and political contingency, thereby propping up the age-old hegemonic practices of domination and control and, simultaneously, masking persisting structural inequalities and propping up the prevailing historical, and neo-colonial privileges.

3 Ontoepistemic Grounding of Contemporary Post-Apartheid Pedagogy

3.1 Introduction

Pedagogy, as Vygotsky (1997) has argued, is never politically indifferent. It has, indeed, always adopted a particular political line in accordance with dominant political ideology of the time which guided its interests. No less so, for the contemporary post-apartheid pedagogy. It is far from being a system premised on values of social justice and equity, and a commitment to redressing historical injustices, as well as the realisation of democratic values that transcends persisting colonial and apartheid inequalities and social injustices. Translating the post-apartheid political ideals of equity and social justice has, not proved an easy task, especially given the deeply rooted structural inequalities that have become deeply entrenched over the four centuries or so of colonial and apartheid regimes. Therefore, these vestiges of past historical and socio-political practices, including the associated socioeconomic structures, revealed themselves in the ideological contestations that followed the collapse of the discredited apartheid regime.

There were two phases through which the post-1994 pedagogical framework evolved. First, there was the failed initial phase of the short-lived Outcomes Based Education (OBE) framework, subsequently replaced by the second phase and the current, neoliberal framework couched, Curriculum Assessment Policy Statement (CAPS). The post-1994 political negotiations resulted in a consensus a give-and-take arrangement that brought about in education, an OBE framework that lasted only the first decade of the post-apartheid democratic dispensation. This, indeed, was a proverbial marriage of convenience, in which contradictory and often discrepant political ideologies coalesced into an uneasy and precarious arrangement. These contradictory political ideologies are in fact manifest in, and through, subsequent ideological contestations that characterised the first decade of the implementation of the post-apartheid pedagogy in the form of the OBE framework. Consequently, these contestations inevitably resulted in the replacement of the OBE framework by the current, relatively more philosophically coherent but yet coercive and hegemonic neoliberal pedagogy.

Therefore, through their underpinning ideological and philosophical grounding, the two versions of the post-apartheid pedagogy inevitably reveal their respective political positionings, with far-reaching implications for societal and human development in South Africa. For example, the OBE framework postulated a worldview underpinned by philosophical eclecticism, a philosophical positioning in which conceptualisation of pedagogy and the associated methodological approaches are randomly picked and packaged to suit the dominant ideology of political reconciliation despite the contradictory political ideologies and the associated incoherent philosophical premises.

3.2 Pedagogy of Convenience

Therefore, in its constructivist approach, the OBE framework emphasised student-centred learning activities and advocated for teachers' minimal intervention. The content of teaching and learning, and the methodologies in which teaching and learning was accomplished, was not rigidly prescribed and teachers were granted the agency to choose the content they deemed most suitable for their specific purposes. The method for teaching was to be carried out within the constructivist framework, which offered most elaborate methodologies for engaging students in constructivist learning. In the constructivist methodology, group work, project work, collaborative learning, exploratory learning, and sharing of ideas through open discussion – with learners interests and goals taken into account – were some of the critical strategies recommended for teaching and learning (Department of Education, 1996).

Additionally, in line with the constructivist approach, the notion of school subjects and the disciplinary boundaries were done away with and replaced by an integrative approach to pedagogy in which related subject disciplines were combined into 'learning areas'. The learning areas were further grouped into 'learning programmes' for the different levels of schooling, with teachers permitted to choose the learning content they deem relevant for their specific students. That is, the choice of the learning content, as well as the order in which this was to be covered during teaching and learning, was delegated to the local level of the school, as the responsibility of communities, parents, teachers, and the students, in accordance with contextual peculiarities and unique learning needs of the students (Department of Education, 1996). This point is important because it was one of the critical grounds on which the OBE framework was critiqued and later replaced by the current CAPS framework, which effectively precluded such local participation both, in its design, as well as its underpinning epistemological grounding.

Therefore, the OBE model encouraged thematic approach to pedagogy, providing opportunities for teachers to connect pedagogy to the needs and interests of their students, including their cultural peculiarities, which the current CAPS approach in its ontological grounding evidently precludes. The thematic approach made it possible for teachers – the few, most competent and agentive teachers at least, to enact self-guided collaborative learning which encourages students to engage with their community, their parents, and siblings, and therefore expand learning to cultural contexts and familiar social settings (see, Muthivhi, 2021). In this way, home and community practices and knowledge traditions are viewed as relevant to advancing learning and development.

However, the OBE framework integrated contradictory philosophical postulations involving the behaviourist approach, in its conceptualisation of knowledge in terms of outcomes. That is, knowledge conceptualised as products, and results of discrete learning experiences. Therefore, pedagogy was defined in experiential terms, as observable outcomes of what learners know and can *do* at the end of their learning *experience* (Department of Education, 1997, my emphasis). Concomitantly, assessment was similarly cast in the same vein, as a means to demonstrate the *observable processes* and *products* of learning, and serving as culminating *demonstrations* of individual learning experiences (Department of Education, 1996).

Indeed, the contradictory philosophical postulations were unfortunate, and resulted in incoherent practices that accounted for much of the confusion on the part of teachers. At the same time, the associated rendering of pedagogy into a process involving artificially connecting students' learning experiences to discrete instances of teaching inputs only reduced classroom practices to mindless mechanical activities. Consequently, teachers became bogged down in petty bureaucratic procedures involving assessing students through painstaking process of connecting individual learning experiences to the discrete instances of the teaching input. Classroom pedagogy was effectively transformed into pyrrhic culture of performative bureaucratic procedures (Department of Education, 2009).

As a result the OBE framework was criticised for overloading teachers with petty administrative activities at the expense of quality teaching and learning. At the same time, the lack of a clearly specified subject content was identified as a fundamental reason for the failure. This omission of content knowledge was considered to have set teachers up for failure since the Black majority teachers were believed to not have the training and the capabilities under the apartheid regime for developing teaching and learning materials on their own (Department of Education, 2009; Jansen, 1999).

Consequently, a commission was appointed to review the OBE framework and to recommend a new framework that would address the continued crisis of school failure. The commission recommended the current framework, named Curriculum Assessment Policy Statement. The new framework was premised on values of self-constrained individualism, pernicious competition, and standardised assessment procedures — with learning conceptualised as a process of adapting to prescribed procedures and predetermined formulas and concepts. There is therefore no room for agency, creativity, and innovation within the CAPS postulation, as teachers and their students are rendered passive, and their activities meaningless and mechanistic, geared at adapting to the status quo of value-neutral and reified concepts. It is this ontological grounding of knowledge and pedagogy on purely epistemic questions, at the expense of an ethical grounding that has undoubtedly characterised contemporary post-apartheid pedagogy and epitomised in CAPS framework. The following section therefore explores such epistemic grounding of pedagogy, to reveal the ontoepistemic basis on which school knowledge and, therefore, pedagogy is predicated.

3.3 Powerful Knowledge versus Knowledge of the Powerful

The concept of powerful knowledge within contemporary post-apartheid pedagogy was derived from the work of the British educational sociologist Basil Bernstein. This concept was translated into the South African educational context through the leading work of Michael Young and Johan Muller (Muller & Young, 2019; Young, 2007). Young (2007) and Muller and Young (2019), for instance, distinguish between 'knowledge of the powerful' and 'powerful knowledge'. According to this point of view, the concept of knowledge of the powerful refers to conceptualisations of knowledge in terms of who controls, defines, legitimises, and prescribes *what* knowledge is that should be part of pedagogy. Consequently, within this framework, dominant socio-economic classes control and define what knowledge is and which knowledge should be prescribed as part of pedagogy. Therefore, the concept of knowledge of the powerful refers to how dominant classes determine what knowledge is that becomes part of pedagogy with the view of catering for their privileged position in society.

In contrast to the concept of 'knowledge of the powerful', Muller and Young (2019) and Young (2007) argue that the concept of 'powerful knowledge' refers to useful knowledge that is not available to students in their home backgrounds and within their spontaneous life situations. This form of knowledge is further defined as 'specialised knowledge' taught by 'specialist teachers', with the goal of schooling being the transmission of such powerful knowledge. As a result, the relations among teachers and their students that arise from a teaching-learning situation that involves powerful knowledge would have specific features. That is, the pedagogical relations, contrary to that which pertains to a constructivist classroom settings, is hierarchical and therefore distinct from peer relations.

Further, and contrary to learning environments informed by constructivist and related progressive epistemologies, pedagogy is not based on students' choice. Nonetheless, Young (2007) argues that the hierarchical relation between teachers and students within the pedagogic situations informed by the concept of 'powerful knowledge' does not necessarily mean that schools should not take the knowledge that pupils bring to the learning situation seriously. According to this view, neither should this suggest that teachers' authority does not need to be challenged. On the contrary, the assumption of hierarchy in the pedagogic relations means that 'some form of authority relations are intrinsic to pedagogy and to schools' (Young, 2007, p. 37).

3.4 Internal Structure of School Knowledge

Young (2007) describes the concept of powerful knowledge in terms of the supposed differences and mutual separation between school knowledge, on the one hand, and the non-school knowledge on the other hand. These differences between school and non-school forms of knowledge are rendered natural and inherent to the respective forms of knowledge and concepts. That is, according to Young (2007), the respective knowledge forms are differentiated by their inherent properties, with school knowledge manifesting as specialised, context-independent, as well as abstract and theoretical. On the contrary, non-school forms of knowledge are identified as concrete and context-dependent. These differences are understood to be inherent to the respective forms of knowledge and their constitutive internal structural dynamics.

Therefore, according to Young (2007), Muller and Young (2019), school knowledge tends to make claims to universality and is associated with the sciences, while non-school knowledge is context-dependent and associated with home and everyday activities that tends to be restricted to the practical and the particular. That is, while school knowledge tends towards generalisations, non-school knowledge tends towards contextual specificities of the here-and-now of everyday activities.

This apolitical and ahistorical activity of validation and legitimation of knowledge and pedagogy, positing it as neutral and disinterested pursuit of facts and formulas devoid of context and human subjectivity. Therefore, knowledge acquisition, and pedagogy is taken to be a universal and value-free process to which students are given access as a means of empowering them to adapt to, and benefit from, the status quo of Western-dominated socio-economic advantages. To this end, the design principles of contemporary post-apartheid pedagogy are revealed. As argued in the review committee's recommendation:

> What we have learnt is that, despite the good intentions of past efforts, an underspecified curriculum advantages those who are already advantaged – those who already have access to the knowledge needed to improve their life chances. What we need to provide is a clear statement of the 'powerful knowledge' (Young, 2007) that provides better learning, life, and work opportunities for learners, especially for teachers who have been dispossessed in the past, who are insecure in the present and uncertain of the future. Certainty and specificity about *what to teach* and *how to teach it* will help to restore

confidence and stability in the system and enhance the learning opportunities we provide for our students. (Department of Education, 2009, p. 62)

Here, the legitimation for discipline-based organisation of school knowledge within contemporary post-apartheid pedagogy is revealed. Therefore, the prevailing circumstances of post-apartheid pedagogy, and the associated socioeconomic conditions, are put forward as grounds for the discipline-based organisation, whilst the plight of disadvantaged Black communities is juxtaposed with better prospects deemed possible only on condition that these communities submit to a pedagogy predicated on the epistemology of 'powerful knowledge'.

3.5 Reified Concepts Devoid of Context

It is therefore in its quest for an objectivist, value-free criteria for the legitimation and validation of knowledge and pedagogy that contemporary post-apartheid pedagogy posits concepts as reified, frozen in time, and devoid of context. Concepts are understood as expanding, and knowledge as growing through some internal dynamic process that is universal and therefore not contingent on context. Young (2007) argues that school concepts and none-school concepts follow different paths that do not collide and are, therefore, dichotomous in their developmental trajectories. Drawing from the work of the British sociologist Basil Bernstein's (2000), Young (2007) and Muller and Young (2019) offer two distinct forms of concept differentiation that happens within the respective knowledge domains of school versus non-school concepts. According to this view, the concept of 'framing' describes the boundaries that are created when students bring non-school knowledge into the classroom, while the concept of 'classification' describes the extent of the differences between knowledge domains, such as between physics and history.

The concept of classification is crucial therefore because it underpins the process through which school knowledge and concepts are differentiated into the various disciplinary orientations. For example, concepts in the domain of the natural sciences, such as physics, are viewed as tending towards vertical progression. That is, concepts in this domain are understood as progressing towards higher levels of abstraction, expanding through a depth process where lower-level concepts are subsumed into higher level ones. The conceptual differentiation therefore establishes a hierarchical structure of scientific knowledge, further determining the methodological procedures for knowledge production and dissemination within the respective knowledge domain. On the contrary, concepts in the social sciences and the humanities, such as in historical disciplines, tend towards horizontal structure, progressing by 'developing new languages which pose new problems' (Muller and Young, 2019; Young, 2007, p. 41).

Herein lies an objectivist rendering of knowledge and concepts into a neutral, value-free process of dispassionate and mentalist knowledge pursuit. The structural dynamics of this knowledge systems and concepts, therefore, favours existing Western canonical epistemologies despite suggestions of a purely neutral and value-free process unfolding by itself, essentially through ostensibly objectivist and universal laws of knowledge and concepts differentiation. This postulation of knowledge and concepts in universalist and objectivist terms, as a process devoid of context and human subjectivity, undoubtedly conceals the deeply rooted hegemonic intent of Western hierarchical and coercive epistemologies. At the same time, the avoidance of political and historical analysis, rendering knowledge, concepts, and pedagogy apolitical and ahistorical processes, only serving the dominant political interests, rendering historical inequities into natural inevitabilities. That is, according to this objectivist epistemology, the world could never be otherwise other *what it is*, cannot be changed in any radical way other than to be acquiescing with. Such is the grounding ethos that underpins the canonical version that demarcates school knowledge into rigid subject disciplines, rendering the process abstract and contemplative – in line with the ideology of adaptation to the status quo of fitting in, and coping with, the pre-established ideas and models, including reified concepts frozen in time.

3.6 The Doctrine of Subject Discipline

The doctrine of subject discipline as the grounding epistemic criteria for knowledge validation within contemporary post-apartheid pedagogy was predominantly derived from the work of leading scholars like Young (2007) and Muller and Young (2019). The subject discipline is therefore considered the substantive part of pedagogy, offering students the opportunity to explore the internal structure of knowledge and 'what the hinterland of the subject has to offer' (Muller and Young, 2019, p. 16). In this postulation, teachers are considered crucial mediators within the 'pedagogical knowledge' of their specific subject areas. When this mediation is successful and students learn successfully, it is then that students can be said to have been empowered in, for example, the quality of judgement, the ability to appreciate the substantial and conceptual fields of the subjects, as well as making new connections and gaining new insights (Muller and Young, 2019).

The postulation of knowledge as defined by properties inherent to its ostensibly objective criteria renders the process of its production and dissemination abstract and solipsistic and, hence, purges the process from the dimension of human subjectivity. That is, students and teachers are positioned as passive, only acquiescing with given conceptualisations and predetermined models and procedures. Consequently, truly creative and innovative contribution becomes impossible, and students' and their teachers' activities become limited to participating by way of adapting to predetermined methodologies and prescribed procedures. Therefore, agentic contribution also becomes impossible to achieve, since the activities are confined to prescribed procedures and methodologies that offer no leeway to connecting knowledge and learning to personal experiences and the practices in culture and society, relevant and significant to students' activities. Pedagogy, within contemporary post-apartheid pedagogy is revealed as cocooned within the artificial parameters of what, in this framework, constitutes as valid and legitimate knowledge rendered in its hegemonic and coercive postulation that strip teachers and students of agency and identity development, transmuting teachers and their students' activities into mindless and inconsequential mechanical processes.

As a result, the development of agency and identity, including the associated processes of connecting knowledge authentically to everyday life practices, interests, desires, and personal goals, is undermined and rendered invalid. These processes are only possible through an approach that connects pedagogy to teachers and students' community practices and associated knowledge traditions. Therefore, a *thematic approach* to pedagogy becomes relevant and absolutely critical. Unfortunately, such an approach is difficult to implement within contemporary post-apartheid pedagogy because of the internal contradiction between the epistemic grounding of the model, vis-à-vis its practical organisation. Therefore, although a thematic approach to pedagogy is recommended for teachers, albeit in contradistinction to the underlying epistemic foundation, the approach is merely recommended for practical application by teachers. The apparent inconsistencies and self-contradictory postulates arising from this recommendation so irked many orthodox scholars that the thematic approach was criticised as entailing 'a superficiality that undermines the credibility of history education' (Kallaway, 2012, p. 58).

3.7 Methods as Inhering in the Discipline

Contemporary post-apartheid pedagogy, premised on coercive Cartesian epistemology that positions humans as passive recipients of orthodox formulations, objective knowledge and reified concepts, prescribes that the methods for pursuing knowledge inheres not on subjective activities of teaching and learning but on the disciplines. That is, the methods for the production and dissemination of knowledge are understood as subject to the internal dynamic structure of the discipline.

According to this view, methodology cannot be connected to the activities of students, and their subjective understanding. Students' engagement with knowledge is understood as inherent in the logic of the subject discipline and therefore not in their subjective learning activities (Department of Education, 2009).

Therefore, contemporary post-apartheid pedagogy is premised on the methodological assumption of incontrovertible authority of disciplinary knowledge, and its associated abstract and mentalist categories. Within this ontological postulation, the methods inhere within the discipline, and are therefore predetermined and independent means for obtaining neutral, universal, and value-free facts about reality. Scientific knowledge and concepts in the natural sciences are posited as tending towards vertical progression and therefore expanding towards context-independent generalisations on the one hand. On the other hand, concepts in the humanities and the arts are posited as following behind their superior counterparts in the sciences, as tending towards horizontal progression and therefore expanding by means of linguistic generalisations. This epistemic grounding of knowledge and pedagogy is premised on the objectivist approach that purges knowledge production from human endeavour. As a consequence, knowledge production is understood as a purely dispassionate process of finding out about the world that exists independently of our goals.

This approach, unfortunately, robs teachers and students of their agentic contribution to knowledge and their own development. That is, knowledge production, including pedagogy, is rendered abstract and mentalistic endeavour of pursuing predetermined answers and solutions to problems within the subject discipline. These solutions and answers are therefore prescribed in, and through, the methods which are, in turn, embedded in and embodied by the subject discipline itself. In a statement that endorses the centrality of the subject discipline and the associated disciplinary knowledge as the centre stage of pedagogic activity, and therefore not the students' own activity, the founding statement spells out the methodological approach of contemporary post-apartheid pedagogy:

> The intention of the National Curriculum Statements was to move towards greater emphasis on discipline-based subjects, the logic of which is derived from the subject discipline. Though all learners do engage in the construction of knowledge in terms of coming to understand certain concepts, skills, and content, it has generally been accepted that all these aspects *inhere within the subject and not within the minds of learners in the first place*. (Department of Education, 2009, p. 24, emphasis added)

Therefore, contemporary post-apartheid pedagogy derives its design principles from the orthodox and canonical postulates of Cartesian epistemologies that proffering a dichotomous worldview of isolated individuals devoid of creativity and innovation, and therefore agency. In this postulation, teachers and their students are positioned as passively adapting to pre-established models and canonical versions of reified concepts, abstract categories, and prescribed procedures. Consequently, rather than encouraging teachers and their students to relate methods to their personal circumstances, conditions, interests, and goals, contemporary post-apartheid pedagogy advances canonical view of methods and pre-established procedures to be emulated and conformed with. This epistemological approach to teaching and learning within contemporary post-apartheid pedagogy extends deep into very core, the procedures of the assessment of students' learning.

3.8 Assessment-Driven Pedagogy

Grounded on objectivist ontology, including the methodological assumptions of isolated individuals, normativity, and hierarchical nature of relational processes, contemporary post-apartheid pedagogy is premised on Western orthodoxies and Cartesian epistemologies that promise absolute certainty, objectivity, neutrality, and certainty (Stetsenko, 2023). These assumptions permeate the assessment practices and form the basis for standardised assessment procedures that prioritises pernicious competition and the associated solipsistic individualism. Assessment within contemporary post-apartheid pedagogy is in fact conceptualised as the fulcrum on which pedagogy evolves. As represented in the founding policy document:

> Government and society in general to measure the quality of the system; to assess the consistency of standards at school and national levels; and to hold schools and teachers accountable for student learning. It also provides signals for employers and higher education institutions about what knowledge future students or potential employees have acquired. (Department of Education, 2009, p. 29)

Therefore, standardised assessment of students' learning and teachers' teaching functions as an instrument of accountability, to ensure that teachers are teaching the prescribed concepts using prescribed methodologies intrinsic to the subject discipline. Assessment, therefore, ensures that pedagogy remains within the confining parameters of what counts as knowledge, and that proper methodologies for the dissemination of subject discipline knowledge are used. In this way, assessment prescribes that students conform to the status quo of passive learning and acquisition of knowledge and concepts, rendered abstract and contemplative. Assessment therefore encourages pernicious individualism and deleterious competition, fashioning teachers and their students into passive recipients of reified knowledge and concepts, objectified and frozen in time.

Therefore, assessment within contemporary post-apartheid pedagogy can be conceptualised as the ultimate coercive instrument that artificially produces false hierarchies while prescribing teachers and their students to passively assimilating concepts and methodologies for reproducing them as correct answers and test results. This positioning of teachers and their students to the incontrovertible authority of disciplinary knowledge, and the associated normativities of standardised assessment procedures, has in fact been quite debilitating within contemporary post-apartheid pedagogy. Such coercive measures have since been emboldened by the recent upsurge of international testing regimes such as TIMMS, driven by what Stetsenko et al., (2025) have called the 'one-size-fits-all normativity of quantitative methodologies of "evidence based research", "brainism", and the unrelenting testing mania in education' (Stetsenko et al., 2025, p. 2). For example, the recent PIRLS results in South Africa[2] have found that Black students in all African languages lag behind their white, English and Afrikaans language counterparts in reading performance, and that by Grade 4 level of schooling, these students cannot 'read with meaning'. The results of these tests are generally accepted uncritically, and solutions are proposed hastily in a simultaneous act of endorsing the results without question. That is, the ecological validity of the tests is not put into question, neither is concept validity vis-à-vis 'reading with meaning' interrogated. This evidently is in line with the coercive agenda of Western orthodoxies, as Cooper (2005) has argued justifies privileges, using the rhetoric of scientific "to sell the idea that historical inequities should be embraced as biological inevitability"' (quoted in, Stetsenko, 2023, p. 30).

One critical issue in regard to the question of ecological validity, especially for Black African students, is the question of language. The subject of language as instructional medium for the majority of South African students is a profoundly complicated matter deeply rooted in historical and sociopolitical conditions of the colonial and apartheid regimes (Muthivhi, 2014, 2008). Language is evidently at the core of the problems that have haunted South Africa's schooling and pedagogy for many years. Therefore, the implications of such undefined concepts as 'reading without meaning', postulated in recent results of the PIRLS test regime could not be any more stifling to a system that sorely requires accurate nomenclature and categorisation. For example, we have found in our studies within indigenous African classrooms (Muthivhi, 2014, 2008) that 'meaning' was

---

[2] See Progress in International Reading Literacy Study – PIRLS (2021). *International Association for the Evaluation of Educational Achievement* (IEA) (2023). TIMMS & PIRLS International Study Center, Lynch School of Education and Human Development, Boston College.

always culturally contingent, while language tended to be used in ways compatible with local traditions of linguistic practices, and could therefore not be rendered universal, value-free, and neutral.

3.9 The Language Dilemma

The postulation of knowledge and concepts as existing outside of subjective experiences, devoid of agency and creativity, is further consolidated, in the design of contemporary post-apartheid pedagogy, through the association of English with conceptual knowledge, on the one hand, while African, indigenous languages are associated with lower level processes involving the acquisition of basic literacy and thinking skills, on the other hand. This coercive and hierarchical positioning in the design of contemporary post-apartheid pedagogy is evidently consistent with the pedagogy's hegemonic postulations.

In its hierarchical rendering of knowledge and the associated processes of knowledge production and its dissemination, English language is elevated to a supreme position as the lingua franca of academic exchange and classroom engagement within African classrooms–including within classrooms where common indigenous African language already exists. The justification for this unfortunate state of affairs, of course, is the purported economic benefits to emanate from emulating Western cultural practices. At the same time, the use of African indigenous languages for academic purposes is postponed to the longue durée of history, and the associated teleology premised on the assumption of the Olympian view of Western culture and civilisation. To this end, language practice within pedagogy is rendered hierarchical, with African languages subservient to colonial language domination, with English and Afrikaans serving such dominant position:

> The thorough development of a child's language skill is a reliable predictor of future cognitive competence. This applies equally to the child's Home Language and Language of Learning. The two languages are in effect two sides of the same coin. While the Home Language plays the primary role in developing literacy and thinking skills and is of importance in enhancing the protection and further development of the indigenous language, the Language of Learning (in particular English) is the one in which students must master educational concepts and provides a platform to participate and engage meaningfully in the information age on a global stage ... We also know that the majority of our learners undergo the majority of their school learning and being assessed in English, as their second language. Crucial attention needs to be paid to issues of language, in particular First Additional Language, English, which remains a strong predictor of student success at school. (Department of Education, 2009, p. 41)

The positioning of teachers and students as devoid of language through which to engage in productive learning activities within South Africa's classrooms is consistent with dominant Western and neocolonial patriarchal viewpoint of African, and other non-dominant communities. According to this view, Africa has contributed nothing of significance to contemporary human achievement, and it continues to linger infantile in need of paternal protection from dominant Western powers. The hierarchical rendering of languages in contemporary post-apartheid pedagogy aligns with global triumph of neoliberal ideology and the underlying capitalist economy that ostensibly benefits colonial language medium pedagogy.

Therefore, Western epistemologies in their Cartesian postulation determine the actual form of pedagogic engagements that should characterise classroom teaching and learning in contemporary post-apartheid pedagogy. That is, in the dichotomous postulation, language is conceptualised as conveyer of knowledge and therefore not as integral part, and the very substance of, and means and end – process and product, of learning and development, including knowledge production practices. According to this postulation, English is presented to be as the predictor of academic success and, as a result, accorded greater attention than the indigenous African home languages.

This hierarchical view of language, as its dichotomous postulation vis-à-vis knowledge and pedagogy, is consistent with the view of knowledge as separate from the process of its production and therefore reified – frozen in time, rather than dynamic, fluid, situated, contingent, and transformative. According to this viewpoint, the future will continue to be the same as the present, and the status quo of Western canons, as well as the associated traditions, define the nature and scope of the present engagements and standards of practice. Therefore, English, as an embodiment of Western culture and the traditions of practice within formal schooling, becomes the natural measure of academic success. As a result, the rich traditions of knowledge embodied by the African indigenous languages, including the associated cultural practices, are, sadly, unfairly excluded from pedagogy. Attendant with this unfortunate methodologies of exclusion, the rich language-based didactic approaches embodied by African languages, such as in the instances of approaches such as *immersion, thematic* approach, d*ramatisation, emotional* connection, and social *interdependence*, as well as the *communal collaborative* approaches, are all dismissed in favour of the approaches that proffer pernicious individualism, deleterious competition, passive adaptation, and the related approaches that render agency, identity, and contingency irrelevant and inconsequential.

3.10 Conclusion

In prescribing coercive and hegemonic criteria for what counts as legitimate and valid forms of school knowledge, contemporary post-apartheid pedagogy, therefore, misses the opportunity to connect knowledge authentically to the realities of students' cultural historical conditions, including conditions that are relevant and significant in students' practical pursuit of life goals and self-identity. That is, in prescribing knowledge only on epistemic criteria, to do with questions of rationality and validity, contemporary post-apartheid pedagogy misses the important opportunity for grounding knowledge, and pedagogy, on ethical values, to do which what is morally correct and just under prevailing historical and political circumstances. That is, a critical missing value in the organisation of contemporary post-apartheid pedagogy comprise of the simultaneous emphasis on how to transform the vestiges of colonial and apartheid schooling by committing to a pedagogy that not only dwells on past coercive and hegemonic epistemic ideals of objectivity and neutrality.

Commitment to future-oriented pedagogy would certainly require ethical grounding of knowledge on moral values of equity and social justice, as a priori categories in the process of knowledge validation and legitimation. Such future-oriented pedagogy implies recognition of the historical injustices of the colonial and apartheid pedagogy, that simultaneously commits to social transformation and agentic self-identity development. This, therefore, is a pedagogy premised on the primacy of ethical dimension of knowledge – as opposed to an epistemological grounding where knowledge is validated only on the basis of its rationality and truth value. Therefore, the ethical grounding of knowledge, as the axiomatic basis for decolonising approach to pedagogy, commits to the debunking of the myths of a purely epistemic grounding of knowledge.

In the ethico-ontoepistemic commitment to a future-oriented approach to pedagogy that does not jettison cultural grounding of human knowledge as the centre stage and core grounding of human life, human beings are not posited as isolated from each other and the world in which they live. On the contrary, this decolonising approach to pedagogy herein postulated proposes an axiological grounding of human being and human development as a profoundly interconnectedness of human individuals who, through their interconnectedness, realise themselves not as isolated individuals but as social and profoundly social agents of their historical development. It is therefore within this ontology of shared and profoundly interconnected world that knowledge production is postulated as embodied and enacted within collective communal practices.

Knowledge is therefore posited as embodied within collective communal practices of culture and society and enacted in the course of collective social practices of which schooling becomes the source and the fulcrum for such collective practices and self-identity development. Knowledge is therefore realised in, and through, collective social practices, with the shared, collective practices taken to be the axiomatic grounding of knowledge production and human development. To this end, Stetsenko, (2023) citing Dewey, explains that no knowledge exists outside the human process of inquiry. That is, '... no concepts, ideas, facts etc.–can be posited to exist outside of inquiry', with the radical connotation that 'inquiry is the very process of which knowledge consists and outside of which no knowledge (in whatever form) exists (Stetsenko, 2023, p. 27).

Therefore, knowledge as enactment of future-oriented contributions to communal practices, not isolated from the methods and instrument of its production, and not devoid of human subjective experiences, inevitably supersedes the Cartesian postulations that underpin contemporary post-apartheid pedagogy. The culturally situated community practices, embodied by students and their teachers and enacted through their traditional performances, are presented in the following section as instantiations of an alternative ontology superseding contemporary post-apartheid pedagogy. That is, in their collective, communal, embodied, and thematic, including performatory approaches, the traditional performances reveal an ethical grounding that supersedes dualist epistemologies and their associated objectivist and solipsistic methodologies. Consequently, this alternative model, dialectically superseding the stifling conditions of the prevailing neocolonial and neoliberal ontology, offers a non-dualist, non-dichotomous, ethically grounded, ideologically imbued, historically contingent, and culturally relevant approach to decolonisng pedagogy. At the same time, such an approach is evidently infused with the moral commitment to social transformation through culturally situated decolonisation approach to pedagogy.

4 Connecting Pedagogy to Culturally Situated Community Practices and Knowledge Traditions

4.1 Introduction

In connecting pedagogy to culturally situated community practices and knowledge traditions, the section presents community practices as instantiated by traditional performances and activities that have survived centuries of systematic exclusion and marginalisation, but continue to exist, though on the margins of mainstream pedagogy within contemporary post-apartheid schooling. That is, the criteria for what counts as valid and legitimate knowledge for schooling in South Africa today continue to preclude culturally situated knowledge traditions and the associated community practices, in favour of methodologies that emphasise abstract, objectivist, and mentalist approaches. Knowledge, according to this viewpoint, is separate from and devoid of subjective experiences of teachers and their students – interests, desires, emotions, and future life goals.

However, in challenging the neoliberal and neocolonial myth of the isolated individual, including the associated values of normativity, neutrality, and objectivity, the decolonising approach to pedagogy herein proposed grounds pedagogy on the principle of profound interconnectedness between human subjectivity, on the one hand, and knowledge production processes, including methodologies by which knowledge is pursued, on the other. In this view, knowledge, and the world, is not viewed as separate, isolated, and independent of human subjective experiences but as indelibly intertwined, intermingled, and deeply infused with human subjective endeavours. Human subjectivity, therefore, is taken to be at the core of, and as the very fabric in the process of knowledge production, itself conceptualised as agentic contributions to future-oriented, culturally situated, communal practices of being-knowing-doing.

That is, positing a model of pedagogy that enables students to recreate events in their community practices and enact them as future-oriented contribution to their social transformation and self-identity development offers a viable alternative to the prevailing epistemologies premised on values espousing normativity, objectivity, and neutrality. As social actors and agents of history, students embody the history of their community practices in which they participate in their quest for realising the world and themselves. Therefore, students enact their agency through communal practices of being-knowing-doing – that is, realising self and contributing to collective social transformation through engaging in practical activities, and thereby acquiring knowledge that is simultaneously grounded on ethical dimension of being human, as opposed to knowledge devoid of ethics and moral values.

Consequently, agency, taken as the core dimension of Being human, with Being, in turn, understood as an event, lived experience – as something that must be lived through than merely perceived – connects students, ethically, to their community practices and culturally situated knowledge traditions. Connecting pedagogy to students' lived experiences, to their culturally situated knowledge practices and traditions, provides an alternative approach to pedagogy grounded not only on epistemic questions but on ethical dimensions of knowledge production, where questions of equity and justice matter and are prioritised.

The proposed stance jettisons quaint epistemologies that position students and teachers as passive and devoid of creativity and innovation, in following with the ideology of adapting to the status quo of objectivity, neutrality, and solipsistic individualism. On the contrary, the proposed model of pedagogy, connecting culturally situated community practices and knowledge traditions, supersedes the dualist epistemologies and their objectivist ontology. That is, the decolonising approach to knowledge and pedagogy, according to this framework, relinquishes coercive and hegemonic methodologies that disguise historical inequities and render Western ethnocentric epistemologies immutable, ubiquitous, and inescapable.

In this emancipatory approach to pedagogy, the ethical grounding of knowledge, prioritising ineluctable unity of human subjectivity, supersedes the epistemic grounding of knowledge production postulated as a process involving the pursuit of objectified knowledge, raw facts, and reified concepts separated from the methods through which they are produced – objectified products devoid of students' agency and life experiences. In the decolonising approach however, the subjective actions of human beings are realised as entailing the ethically grounded process of being-knowing-doing, enacted within the profound interconnectedness of their morally grounded deeds, within the dynamics of culture, history, and identity, and as involving a process of 'becoming-through-doing' (Stetsenko, 2007, p. 754). In their enactment, therefore, the culturally situated community practices and knowledge traditions are instantiated by 'traditional' performances. The performances are, however, only perceived to be 'traditional' on the specific consideration of their embodiment of the past history and cultural heritage of community practices which have nonetheless continued to survive and flourish in communities, as well within the contemporary post-apartheid pedagogy, notwithstanding the exclusionary consequences of neo-colonial epistemologies.

Therefore, knowledge and concepts are revealed in their process of production, at the same time, students and their teachers realise themselves and the world as they desired it to be. That is, students realise themselves as agentic contributors who matter, in their sought-after world-in-the-making, which they realise, that is, 'make real', in the here-and-now of contributing to knowledge through an ethically grounded process of becoming-through-doing.

In this dialectical process of superseding the dualist postulation of knowledge, reified, frozen in time, and canonised within the Cartesian methodologies and their associated hegemonic epistemologies, knowledge is posited as culturally situated, and embodied in culturally situated community practices and knowledge traditions which students enact during their learning and development. Consequently, teachers participate in the creation of emotionally intense learning and developmental conditions or learning events through which their students realise their culturally situated community practices and knowledge traditions in their authentic connection to classroom pedagogy. The notion of supersedence therefore comes alive in the context of an authentic connection of knowledge and pedagogy to students' culturally situated community practices and knowledge traditions, and the postulations that characterised neocolonial and neoliberal pedagogy cease to exist in their dichotomy, also losing their condition of hybridity. The concept of 'supersedence' is important in the current, decolonising approach in that the narrow epistemic confines of the cognitivism and objectivism are superseded by ethically grounded postulation, as indelibly intertwined with and, profoundly interconnected to students and teachers' practical purposes, end-goals, including the associated moral visions for social transformation and self-identity development. That is, as Stetsenko (2020a) has explained in specific regard to the history of knowledge, the dialectical sense of superseding older views involves including them at the next step within newly developed, higher level conceptualisations. That is, the problematic areas in the theory and its associated models are negated, at the same time that powerful dimensions are integrated – or, to be more precise, *subsumed* into more developed, higher-level conceptualisations.

4.2 Sociodramatic Play (*Mahundwane*)

As a culturally situated community practices and knowledge tradition revealed through students' participation in their community practices, the sociodramatic *mahundwane* (or *maotlwane*) plays a vital role in children's development and learning. Children acquire the values and norms of their society and culture through taking up and enacting the roles of adults in a play situation that recreates the very practices they observe but are not fully able to participate in as adult members of society. The sociodramatic, mahundwane play, therefore, enables children before adolescent stage to enact the roles of adults and by doing so, enter the roles and experience the emotions of, as well as acquire and practice the values and norms expected from adult members of society. However, the rules that children recreate may not apply in the strict manner in which they are often encountered in community practices, and may therefore be renegotiated, revised, and changed in accordance with the unfolding goals and purposes of children participating in the play activity. Children, therefore, exercise free will – personal volition and, hence, their agency as free members of their society in full control of their own learning and development.

Therefore, mahundwane sociodramatic play has far-reaching implications for how human development and learning could be realised within the sociocultural settings that are most conducive and free of constraints. That is, sociocultural settings free of the constraints such as characterised by coercive values fashioned along dominant socio-economic interests, conceptualised as the inevitable future and, hence, tacitly supposing that the future will always be the same as the present.

The developmental consequence of mahundwane play is clear, in that children participate in activities for which they are responsible for the organisation, and they therefore also participate in creative and innovative activities of planning, reflecting on outcomes and possible consequences of their actions while enacting roles that simultaneously require following rules, including adapting the rules in a quest for advancing the viability of play as a collective activity with shared responsibilities. Therefore, children participate in activities that require abstraction of concrete relations in their home and community background, while engaging in activities that require abstraction and generalisation of knowledge and concepts, hence reflecting on, and learning about, themselves and their community practices. During mahundwane play, children perceive the shared, dynamic world in which phenomena are interconnected and interdependent and therefore not rendered dichotomous and oppositional.

Children develop strong emotional disposition and interpersonal relationships, and learn to value others and the contributions they make in regard to the common purpose, solidarity, and collective good. Therefore solidarity and common, collective values of togetherness, as opposed to values underpinned by self-interested individualism and deleterious competition, are developed and internalised as part of the qualities and personalities of children growing up in environments where mahundwane sociodramatic play activity is an integral part of social and cultural values. At the same time, children acquire concepts about the social world as inevitably connected with, rather than oppositional to, the natural environment, as well as the related concepts of the profound interconnectedness of human experiences, knowledge, and events unfolding in society and in the natural world. Children therefore acquire a culturally situated understanding of the ambiguities and contradictions of social relations enacted in, and through their home and community practices. This understanding is revealed not through isolated and cognitivist pursuit of solipsistic endeavours, but by practical and agentic engagement in, and contribution to, community practices and knowledge traditions embodied by the mahundwane sociodramatic play.

Mahundwane sociodramatic play therefore presents teachers with the opportunity to connect pedagogy to culturally situated community practices and knowledge traditions, thereby creating a new learning event for students to transform classroom activities into personal pursuit of meaningful goals. That is, the knowledge embodied by mahundwane sociodramatic play activities, and the associated organisational procedures, could be transformed into meaningful tools for the pursuit of literacy skills, including the skills necessary for the development of scientific and mathematical knowledge and concepts. The critical-analytic, exploratory, and imaginative skills children develop through mahundwane sociodramatic play activities can be transformed into tools for personal pursuit of knowledge and concepts in the classroom, in social studies, science learning, as well as in mathematics. Therefore, mahundwane sociodramatic play provides culturally situated knowledge practices which students could transform into tools for pursuing their learning and development. For instance, students perceive the consequences of the historical and sociopolitical structures, and the contradictory relations that characterise everyday life conditions in their society and schooling.

Mahundwane sociodramatic play therefore provides what Vygotsky (1978) has termed the 'pre-history' of developmental processes, and in this case, mahundwane provides the pre-history of the development of concepts within schooling. That is, the concepts of number, measurement, as well as the associated concepts involved in the notion of metric system – such as length, volume, weight – can be revealed in this pre-history, as embodied by culturally situated community practices and enacted by students as goal-oriented activities of society and culture. The purposes for which measurements are used, as well as how they are actually applied in practice, are all imbued by human purposes and can therefore be revealed in the course of human pursuit of personal goals and purposes. Arievitch and Stetsenko (2000) provide an account of how the concept of measurement was actually revealed to students through practical engagement with culturally situated knowledge practices, and as grounded on personal pursuit of concrete solutions to real-life problems and, therefore, as evolving through such mundane strivings and struggles geared towards finding solutions to everyday life concerns.

4.3 Traditional Indigenous Games

Indigenous games could be utilised to provide students with critical tools for self-reflection and planning, and therefore engender skills such as manipulating qualitative relations, estimating quantity, and more critically developing social and emotional skills, and the associated values of solidarity, responsibility, including care for others as a moral condition of being human. Traditional games are revealed as a form of community engagement through practices that transform everyday activities and render them into pastimes that serve to build solidarity and social harmony. While traditional games carry important didactic value for players, what is often emphasised is not the skills and the sportsmanship displayed but the companionship, social harmony, solidarity, and shared communal values that are encouraged and enhanced through participation in the games.

Traditional indigenous games are played within as well as across the age groups and are therefore an important way of initiating young players into the values of their society, at the same time that critical social skills and dispositions are promoted. There are games suited for younger-age children to play among themselves and these are usually more simplified than those intended for adults, although adolescents are generally deemed old enough to partake in adult games. Since games have their history in social practices and simultaneously reflect on, even critical to, those practices that they serve to instil socially accepted values while discouraging conduct that is not socially acceptable.

Just as in the case of the sociodramatic mahundwane play, traditional indigenous games have important developmental consequences for children and young people growing up in African societies such as responsibility, social and emotional maturity, as well as strong moral values and people-oriented skills. These are fundamentally important skills that speak to the moral vision and ethical grounding of children and young people's cultural life world. At the same time, these values and ethical grounding of the activities involved in traditional indigenous games supersede the more practical skills such as number manipulation and quantitative competence, which the games inevitably promote among the players albeit indirectly.

Therefore, grounding pedagogy on ethical dimension has the advantage of creating opportunities for students to transform their embodied knowledge into tools for personal pursuit of self- knowledge, identity development, and, therefore, agentic contribution to social transformation and self-identity development. That is, culturally situated knowledge practices embedded in the games, and embodied by the students, is taken as grounding the learning and development that unfolds during classroom pedagogy and therefore situate the pedagogic activities whereby students are rendered competent and successful learners. The teacher guides the students through the activities and thereby makes possible that the concepts of, for example, number relations, quantitative manipulations, which they are already performing in their play activities are revealed to them as concepts that are not only abstract and devoid of context. On the contrary, the concepts are revealed to students as concrete and practical, as well as abstract and conceptual at one and the same time. That is, the conceptual knowledge embedded in students' culturally situated activities, embodied by them, and enacted as pedagogic events, is transformed into meaningful procedures, categories, and methods for the pursuit of self-knowledge and identity development. Consequently, the game of *mufuvha* below, illustrates this conceptual transformation of culturally situated knowledge practices into meaningful tools for personal pursuit of knowledge, including the pursuit of meaningful learning and development.

4.3.1 Board game – Mufuvha

Mufuvha is a board game widely played across much of South Africa, including many parts of Africa. The structure of the game is organised as involving strategies such as cattle-raiding practices between traditional communities, common during pre-colonial Africa. Embodied in the structure of the game are practical skills such as the estimation of quantity, decision-making, tactical skills, and strategies for out-playing opponents, thereby, gaining tactical advantage over opponents.

Mufuvha board game is played on a wooden board, hardened earth surface, or stone surface curved into four rows of capsule holes which serve to hold the stone tokens or counters for playing the game. The game is played by two or more players, or a whole group of players, on opposing sides, with the opposing groups contributing ideas and concrete strategies and thereby taking collective action in support of their respective lead players. One of the critical goals of this activity is to outwit the other player in regard to the skill of estimation of quantity of counters in each hole, and in relation to where each batch of counters would terminate when each token is placed anticlockwise into each of the holes targeting the opponents' hole that contains the most tokens.

The counters – *thoga* in the adult version of the game comprises up to twenty-eight holes divided into two rows each for the opposing groups, while a simpler version of the game played by younger boys below adolescence stage consists of only one counter per hole and two counters on the far-left side of each player. In the adult game, each of the two sets of capsule holes, consisting of 6 up to 112 holes, and played with up 218 counters. Each of the inner raw holes on the far-left side closest to each player remains empty, and the holes adjacent to these contain only one counter each. The empty holes on the far-left end of each player are reserved for the storage of captured counters, and these may be increased to four holes in the case of a larger 112 holes and over 218 counter boards.

Deciding on who starts the game may be done by throwing the dice, and the play proceeds by way of each player placing one counter, one hole at a time anticlockwise. When the last token is deposited into the last hole against the opponent's raw with counters, those counters are captured and added into the loot, kept in the far-left capsules reserved for this purpose – an empty bowl can also be used as in Figure 1. The player proceeds playing until he or she ends at the empty opponent's row – or empty self-raw – and the opponent then takes over and proceeds in the same way. The play may proceed until one player has only one counter, which he is forced to deposit into the adjacent hole and thereby forced to end the game when this last counter is captured. The game is won when the opponent's counters have all been captured.

Figure 1 Mufuvha board game.

There are no bad feelings manifested during the course of play, and magnanimity of spirit supersedes acts of outwitting each other. Creativity and innovation associated with quantitative manipulation, including foreplaning and good judgement, are promoted in and through the activities of the game. At the same time, these skills are subsumed in the grounding values of social harmony, solidarity, and collective responsibility.

4.3.2 Pebble Tossing Game – Ndode

Ndode, pebble tossing game, is normally played by girls, usually before adolescence stage and involves tossing a pebble up, often by the right hand – supposing the player is right-handed of course – with the goal of catching it on its downward fall. The game may be played with one hand, or two hands where the left hand in case of right-handed players may be used to scoop the batch of pebbles from inside the circle or capsule, also ensuring that all pebbles are swivelled back again into the circle on the next throw as the player fast intercepts the tossed pebble on its downward descent. If the player misses and therefore fails to pick the descending pebble, she has lost the game and another child takes over. Only one hand, the right hand – or left hand if the player is left-handed – is used for pebble throwing. Throwing the pebble up again will then lead to the scooping of the bunch of pebbles inside the capsule out, or back into the capsule again, with the goal remaining the successful capture of the tossed pebble on its downward spiral into the circle. The player must always make sure that one or two pebbles – whichever is the level of play – has been left out or else must repeat the throwing so as to leave the right amount of pebbles outside for the bounty. The player continues to play so long as the tossing pebble has not been dropped and the opposing player will take the pleasure of appreciating to skill of concentration and motor coordination.

The game proceeds and the opposing player takes over when the tossing token has been dropped, and the game proceeds likewise. The winning player will be the player with the most counters, and the winning player is duly celebrated by all for the achievement. The girls complement each other generously, as the end goal of the game is always that of companionship, solidarity, and cooperation. The motive during play is always one of reciprocity of action underpinned by ethos of collaboration. The practical skills of concentration, attention span, quantitative manipulation, and so on are subsumed under the ethical values of building friendship, cooperation, and emotional development.

4.3.3 Emotional Pebble Grinding Storytelling Game -Masekitlana

Masekitlana, emotional storytelling game, literally meaning 'let us beat each other', is an emotional re-enactment of events and experiences in home and community practices, where the different social roles represented in the various social events are narrated in the story line, with a focus specifically focused on emotional intensity of the experiences in the events. The game is often played by young pre-adolescent girls who narrate their emotional experiences of everyday life within their home and community settings. The game is normally played at the conclusion of the day, or may be played at intervals between other games or play activities. The game, therefore, involves a group of children deciding to play the make-believe-storytelling game, identified by the grinding of a hand-size stone against a larger grinding stone, as if grinding on a traditional grain hand mill. A home and community environment made up of representational pebbles is recreated, and the represented figures are used in the story as symbolising social roles of mother, father, uncle, teacher, and so on.

Masekitlana storytelling game is therefore a miniature form of *mahundwane* sociodramatic play, differing by its emphasis of, and specific focus on, the narration of personal experiences by individual player who enacts the intense emotional experiences in a storytelling role-play event. The social roles are represented by stones and other related objects which are positioned near the player so she could refer to the relevant social actors as she narrates the events, satirise, and critiques the social roles adults in her context play, relative to her practical experiences of the events within the home and community practices.

The game begins with a group of girls inviting each other to play, and picking up the stones, usually collected into pouches consisting of the creatively converted front materials of the attires. The stones are each allocated roles such as father, mother, neighbour, visiting cousin, and so on. Then the girls assume convenient positions where soft soil can represent a homestead with huts, courtyards, and pathways sculptured on the soft ground. Then, the game is played by one girl at a time, enacting her emotional experiences in the form of a story, emphasising intense emotional impact of the events by grinding even harder with greater emotional intensity, as if grinding grain on a traditional stone mill. The more emotionally intense the story, the more audience connection and acknowledgement it receives. The player would then continue with the narration. The increasing intensity with which the story is told attracts even more audience from the other girls who would abandon their own stories to congregate around the performer they deem most compelling. Such a performer will, in turn, perform the story with even more intensity on the realisation that the audience is attracted to her performance.

Josep et al. (2014) describe masekitlana in the context of pretend-play in which children acquire symbolic abilities associated with the developmental stages proposed in the Piagetian and Vygotkian frameworks respectively. On the contrary, masekitlana should perhaps be understood within an ontology that goes beyond rigid stage theory postulations within Western orthodoxies. That is, rather than postulated as a circumscribed period and an the activity of the child that is limited by the specific developmental stage into which — and out of which, children grow, and ultimately leaving it behind, masekitlana should be viewed through the prism of the profound interconnectedness of human beings, with children recreating social roles and experiencing these roles through their critical engagement with them and hence, creating their own development – rather than adapting to adult roles and through this adaptation, acquiring the skills of their society and culture. In this postulation, children acquire knowledge by transforming their culturally situated community practices into embodied knowledge, which they enact as part of their contribution to social transformation and, hence, self-identity development. That is, rather than viewed only as a form of growing up into, and acquiring pre-existing norms and values, including stating, immutable, and reified knowleldge and skills, masekitlana should essentially be conceptualised as culturally situated knowledge practices enacted by children as authentic contribution to social transformation and, hence, self-development and identity.

Masekitlana emotional storytelling games may, therefore, be recreated into pedagogic events where children may experience the freedom of learning, where they exercise their will, and have agentic control of their knowledge. That is, children's agency, which involves their ability to be creative and innovative, is emphasised, and their intense emotional experiences within community practices are transformed into foundations for their learning and development. In this way, knowledge, and concepts, is revealed to students through their activities, embedded in their community practices, as well as embodied and enacted by them as tools for meaningful pursuit of self-knowledge and identity. Further, culturally situated knowledge practices embodied by students and embedded in the various forms of performance traditions are revealed with immanent force through the musical heritage of the *Domba* school's 'rumbling mountain snake' performance, *tshikona* – 'Abdim's storks reed-pipe wind dance performance', as well as the *tshigombela* – 'rooster mating ritual dance performance'.

4.4 Musical Heritage

Nowhere is the notion of human entanglement with nature, and the profound interconnectedness of humanity vis-à-vis knowledge and human subjectivity, revealed with immanent force than in, and through, the culturally situated community practices and knowledge traditions embodied by students and enacted by them in the pursuit of self-realisation and social transformation. In this understanding, the shared collective social practices are taken as the axiomatic grounding of knowledge, and knowledge is understood as realised through the profound human interconnectedness who, through their interconnectedness, realise themselves as agents of their society and culture. Therefore, the shared and profoundly interconnected world is postulated as the axiomatic grounding of Being and becoming and, hence, knowledge production, is conceptualised as agentic contribution to collective communal practices.

Therefore, rather than unfolding as solipsistic and mentalist endeavour lacking history and context, the process of knowledge production, and pedagogy, is posited as profoundly agentic, culturally situated, and historically contingent. That is, knowledge practices and production reveal particular historical political struggles taking place in society and is, therefore, not conceptualised as a neutral, apolitical and ahistorcal endeavour. That is, knowledge is revealed as a process of mutual embedding, of collective communal practices, including processes in nature, into an indelible unity of being human, including human becoming. Consequently, the culturally situated community practices and knowledge traditions manifest through the various performance traditions, such as the domba, tshikona, and tshigombela, reveal this embodiment of knowledge and its simultaneous enactment within community practices as well as in schooling practices. At the same time, embodied knowledge practices embedded in culturally situated performance traditions, can be meaningfully connected to classroom pedagogy. In this way, students are guided in the exploration of knowledge and concepts within schooling, with the dynamic conceptual relations and the contradictory epistemic postulations revealed in, and through, students' practical exploration and meaningful engagement with reality.

4.4.1 Domba *School: Rumbling Mountain Snake Performance*

Traditionally the *Domba* is associated with highest form of traditional schooling which culminates the various stages in the didactic process where young people were initiated into the knowledge and skills, as well as the norms and values of their society. In the past, domba school lasted up to six years, preceded by a number of individual pre-adolescent schools for boys and girls. These forms of traditional schools were gradually replaced by modern Western schooling, although the traditional performances associated with traditional schooling outlived the colonial onslaught. Even more importantly, these performances continue to be actively enacted by young people in their communities and within formal school settings, and the young people are often guided by their teachers and community members, although they also take responsibility for teaching each other on their own.

According to tradition, Domba school brings together whole communities and is normally conducted when all members of community could attend and participate in the events, conducted in the open *khoro* courtyard where important community meetings are conducted. It is a community practice par excellence. The roles are divided according to levels of performance expected of the participants. Only boys who have graduated from the male *Thondo* school could attend and participate in the Domba. Meanwhile, only girls who have graduated from the numerous puberty schools for girls and are now adolescents, ready for advanced instruction on the knowledge and social skills, including norms and values of their society could be enrolled into the Domba school. Girls who at adolescence would not have completed the numerous pre-Domba schools would not attend the Domba school until they complete the previous stages of the traditional schooling system.

The organisation of Domba, as well as the associated hierarchical structure of the performance events, has close resemblances with the social organisation and role responsibilities within communities, especially as pertaining to the students taking responsibilities for each other and collaborating in the execution of complex performances that require absolute concentration and cooperation by each individual member. A male and female adult members represent the authority of the Domba school, and are assisted by select girls and boys who have distinguished themselves as diligent students during the previous school sessions. The *Nemungodzwa*, male principal, is generally responsible for male students, while the *Nematei (Nyamatei)*, 'mother of domba', female principal, takes care of female students. The already graduated boys and girls assistants serve as tutors for the students – or *vhatei*. Female tutors are responsible for the day-to-day care of female students, while male tutors take care of the male students. Issues such as menstruation and provision of required provisions, as well as the responsibilities for emotional support, are taken care of by the tutors who take pride in carrying these responsibilities.

The students are adorned in special attire, namely, the *thuthu* beaded waist belts, with pieces of white broken sea shells and white ostrich eggs, nowadays often replaced by cotton material sewn into white balls. The girls' costumes represent the high status the students have assumed by successfully completing prior puberty and early adolescence schools to reach the current stage. During the course of the domba, students go through various lessons about the complexities and ambiguities of adult life and how they should rely on their good judgement and wisdom as autonomous members of society. That is, students are taught about communal values such as: for the community to endure, their individual contribution as adult members of society remains critical. Consequently, critical learning events are presented to students by way of dramatisation, while different clay and wood-crafted objects symbolising events in community practices, while the moral dilemmas of adult life are presented to the students in the form of questions and riddles posed for the students to resolve on their own. Solutions to the puzzles and life dilemmas posed to students are never fully resolved for them but left for them to continue to ponder about, representing real-life dilemmas which require individual engagement and resolution, based on the moral vision of a viable life presented to the students through the various thematic lessons presented during the prolonged activities of the domba school (Blacking, 2007, 1995a, 1995b, 1971, 1970; Schutte, 1978; Stayt, 1931; Van Warmelo, 1989).

At the beginning stages of the domba school, students learn to perform the intricate steps involved in the performance of the long *deu* chain movement comprising of students, led by the tutors and the principals. The main domba musical performance involves students with arms holding each other forming a single row of unbroken *deu* chain. The slow elegant movement begins with the beating of the big drum in staggered tempo, with the deep sound of the drum complemented by the slow chanting of words of the main ceremonial song by the female principal, to which the students respond in chorus *'ahee-ahee'*, indicating agreement and solidarity with the tone and mood of the event. The tutors guide students on the intricacies of the domba movement. The students' movement begins by the shoving of the left elbow as the students face the inside of the anticlockwise *deu* movement towards the drummers, with heads dropped down. The girls thrust their arms upwards, and slowly pushing the arms forward and backward twice, coordinating with the simultaneous movement forward of the left leg. The movement is repeated on turning the upper body to the opposite direction, outside of the *deu* file, thus creating an elegant gliding movement of the 'rumbling mountain snake'. See Figures 2 and 3 for an illustration of *deu* procession in a slow-paced and fast-paced domba performances respectively. Also see Video 1 and Video 2 below for a slow paced 'great song of Domba' and the fast paced 'minor song of Domba', respectively.

After a prolonged period of gradual, slow-paced elegant performance of the great song of domba, praising the mountain snake that rumbles deep within, in the womb, the *deu* movement begins to move faster and faster until its peak, especially towards the end of the ceremony, when the pace would often end with a much faster-paced *deu* chain movement. With the elegant but yet heightened pace of the *deu* chain, the 'mother of domba' female principal symbolic rendition becomes even more unequivocal with explicit references to the rumbling snake, the snake that thunders in my womb[3] (Blacking, 1971), and

Figure 2 A performance of the great song of *Domba*. Video file available at www.Cambridge.org/Muthivhi

---

[3] See also, Blacking, John. 2002. Domba 1956-1958: A personal record of Venda initiation rites, songs & dances. VHS tape. (Number 2), www.ethnomusicology.org/store/viewproduct.aspx?id=1237959

Figure 3 A performance of the fast-paced minor song of *Domba*. Video file available at www.Cambridge.org/Muthivhi

'*muololi*' — penis, the mountain snake that rumbles, and the injunction to 'growling young men never to crush me like falling stone houses of *Dzata* kraal' (Nemapate, 2010, p. 88). The great song of domba; about the rumbling mountain snake is therefore considered most sacred, epitomising the various didactic themes covered during the students' long stay at the domba school. In, and through, the great song of domba, the teachings of domba school are recreated and enacted thematically as the gradual transformations of concepts and values, into a bodily form and, simultaneously, embodying the transformations of the life cycle, symbolising collective responsibility demanded by, and centred on, the ambiguities and intricacies of sexual life, copulation, and the collective responsibilities beginning with the early, embryonic forms of life through to the cultural future of communal responsibilities (see also, Blacking, 1971, 1970).

The theme of fertility represented by the python, the mountain snake that rumbles, is actually well known among young people and is encountered early in life through the *ngano* fireside stories – also included in many elementary school readers in South Africa. In traditional ngano fireside stories, the python appears as eligible bachelor who is nonetheless rejected by the bride to be, leading to sudden failing of crops, forests dying out rivers, and water pools drying up. The calamity is ended when the snake is appeased by means of human sacrifice. In another story, the python appears as 'the ever-sleeping one' who is loath to enter, and remains in the dumpsite for fear of the mother. The story, which is also performed as a folk song, ends with the bride urging the groom to come nonetheless, even suggesting that the python considers striking her obstinate mother in the case she insists on denying entry (Blacking, 1995b; Nemapate, 2010; Schutte, 1978; Stayt, 1931).

There are important didactic and pedagogic implications in the thematic approaches of the domba school, including the dramatisation, and performatory approaches to pedagogy embedded in the *matano* – 'exhibitions' or the *ngoma* – drum or profound programme of teaching and learning. The lessons of domba are therefore presented in the form of special events or occurrences that are presented in dramatic form and enacted by the students themselves under the guardianship and tutelage of the 'mother of the domba' principal. The ngoma lessons are presented thematically, with the emphasis on performatory contribution to the collective and therefore literally meaning 'dancing to the beat of the big drum'. In a detailed exposition of the various ngoma performatory didactic events, Nemapate (2010), in an unpublished study, details up to twenty events which are performed, each at a time over the long, up to six year span of the domba school – in the original pre-colonial version of the domba school. These various ngoma events, therefore, demand that the didactic activities assume a thematic approach to knowledge, thereby connecting the lessons to the students' life experiences, vis-à-vis their projected future life goals. The didactic approach therefore never prioritises existing knowledge and skills, although these are taught, but emphasizes the values and attitudes which the students would require as they face challenges of complex and often unpredictable future as adult members of their society.

At the same time, within the ngoma events, students are also presented with the *matano* exhibitions, or revelations, made out of clay and wooden artefacts. These events, meant to be observed, and the performance activities meant for students' participation have crucial symbolic value and embody students' intense emotional experiences which no doubt will remain with them their entire lifetime. After that, students are encouraged to observe an event which is enacted before them; they are subsequently asked questions such as: What is it you have observed", or "What do you deem this to represent"? Interestingly, the resolution to the posed question is not emphasised and the teacher may not probe the answers further or validate the correctness and truth value of the proposed answers or solutions. The moral value, and associated cultural meanings the events and the artefacts embody, is what is considered important. The ethical, as opposed to the epistemic, is considered fundamental for the students' acquisition of the moral attitudes and ethical values of their society. For example, in one of the ngoma dramatisations, a clay calabash containing traditional beer is exhibited to the students for them to observe and tell the domba teachers what it is they are observing. After the exhibit, the calabash is thrashed on the floor to break and spill the white content (Blacking, 1995b; Nemapate, 2010; Schutte,

1978; Stayt, 1931). For example, in this dramatic event, what is manifest, and revealed by the enactment, is the social significance of fertility, and procreation, while its fragility is also revealed to the students at one and the same time.

4.4.2 Tshigombela: *Rooster Mating Ritual Performance*

Unlike the ceremonial domba performance, *tshigombela* is a high-tempo earthbound performance similar to the many performances that characterise the pre-domba puberty schools that culminate in admission to domba school. Tshigombela performance is sharp and rapid, in the manner of the *pre-domba matangwa*–'enactments' or 'drama', where young girls perform highly complex and demanding physical activities showcasing physical maturity. Tshigombela is played by adolescent girls and, in contrast with the boys' *Tshikanganga*, tshigombela is earthbound, has a fast tempo with hard stomping of ground, and is accompanied by energetic singing and beating of the tempo and alto drums. The boys' tshikanganga, in contrast, is leisurely and airborne in the manner of *tshikona*, and is only played on wind-blown reed pipes with no vocal rendition.

Tshigombela is a girls' pre-adolescent performance, characteristic of the many mockery songs played by boys and girls, where they ridicule and satirise each other's roles. Mockery occurs in boys and girls songs as a form of artistic skill and an accepted form of self-expression. For example, Blacking (1995a) describes a girls' song in which a rooster is mocked for wanting to mate with a hen. Similarly, an unpublished study (Nemapate, 2010, p. 79) describes a mockery song performed during *Tshifase* performance where boys and girls mock each other using cock and hen symbolisms. In this performance, girls sing about a cock wanting to mate, while boys sing back referring to female chickens, with the solo couple performing a mating ritual dance.

Tshigombela performance is therefore a girls' enactment of 'roosters' mating ritual dance', generally performed by young pre-adolescence and early adolescence girls adorned in special domba format costumes at waist level but male type attire on the upper body. The dance involves intricate steps symbolic of roosters' mating, including representations of natural phenomena, weather changes and climatic conditions (Muthivhi, 2021). Tshigombela performers enter the arena singing in a single file, walking round the alto and tenor drums which are placed at the centre and accompany the singing. The dancers perform the *u losha* tribute gesture, going down on one side of their body facing the inside of the anticlockwise procession. On raising up, the performers trot in anticlockwise file, with their bodies bent to the inside of the circle towards the drummers, continuing with the singing, with their heads dropped to the inside of the circle.

The initial slow paced anticlockwise movement changes to a much faster, energetic tempo, with earthbound intricate steps involving one leg to the inward direction where their bodies bed, while the other leg to the right remaining outside and lifting up away from the inside of the circle. The right hand is also half-stretched towards the inside while the left one outstretches high towards the outside, swivelling around and flighting bright handkerchiefs or white towels. The movement grow much faster akin to a violent gust of tropical elements, with the atmospheric conditions evoked by the energetic blowing of whistles, high pitched singing voices, and swivelling of bright coloured materials, as well as the vehement swinging of hands–including swivelling of left hand and occasionally hanging the hand on the backside like the rooster's wing and body posture positioned sideways. See figure 4 below for an illustration of the tshigombela performance. Below, lso see Video 3: young Girls performing Tshigombela.

Tshigombela therefore embodies cultural values and provides children with the opportunity to acquire such values through their participation in and–simultaneously, contributing to culturally situated community practices and knowledge traditions. Young girls clearly take up and embody the roles provided in and through *tshigombela* performance, which they enact in their personal, yet culturally situated, pursuit of self-meaning and identity development. These, obviously, are the culturally situated community practices and knowledge traditions that– when meaningfully and authentically connected to pedagogy, would inevitably transform it and render students' performance ethically grounded and successful.

Figure 4 Young girls performing *Tshigombela*. Video file available at www.Cambridge.org/Muthivhi

The epistemic topics involving such subject matter as climate change, weather conditions, as well as the associated subjects involving atmospheric circulation, including the earth's underlying physical processes, can obviously be elaborated as ethically grounded knowledge postulates that authentically connect to students' practical realities and real-life conditions.

4.4.3 Tshikona: *Abdim's Storks Reed-pipe Wind Dance Performance*

The stately airborne 'Abdim's storks wind dance performance', accompanied by a symphony of reed pipe music played by a large group representing the community comprised of all ages, from the youngest able to blow the pipe to the oldest member of still able to blow the pipe and perform white-bellied 'Abdim's storks wind dance' steps. *Tshikona* is therefore organised as a whole *community event,* with each performer playing a single reed pipe set on set of flutes played on seven – note heptatonic scale. The seven *mutavha* flutes represent each age band – '*mirole',* as determined in accordance with tradition. Each set of these flute pipes representing an age band, therefore, produces a tonal structure that forms a composite rhythmic structure, and each pipe within the set, in turn, represents a unique and individual contribution to the collective performance.

Tshikona is stately performance and is performed in various important communal events, including especially the celebration of the first fruits *thevhula* ceremonies. Like all performances discussed above, tshikona is performed in anticlockwise direction. The anticlockwise direction is significant in its association with the south easterly trade winds, responsible for precipitation during spring and summer seasons. For example, the historical significance of the *mbedzi* southeasterly trade winds in the socioeconomic activities and cultural organisation of northeastern South Africa's traditional communities is well documented (Ralushai, 1977; Ralushai and Gray, 1978). In associated ethnographic reports, Blacking (1995b), for example, reports on white-bellied Abdim's storks wind dance, to which boys would chant that the maovhelwa storks are performing tshikona. Abdim's storks dance is particularly special because they *'tanga'* tshikona – a specific mode of dancing associated with elders or stately persons of high rank who reluctantly join the performance at its climax – in the manner of 'u tanga', thus endorsing the performance, but withdrawing early to leave the performers proceed in the stately fashion which the elder has endorsed through 'u tanga' form of dancing. Further, Abdim's stocks prey on locusts and army worms and were therefore regarded, within traditional communities, as protectors of crops, and were also associated with ancestors who returned every year to protect the welfare of their descendants (Blacking (1995b, p. 101; see also, van Warmelo, 1989). Figure 5 illustrates the teacher teaching the wind dance steps of Tshikona to his students, while Figure 6 illustrates a community performing Tshikona. Below, see Video 4.

Figure 5 A lesson about the performance of *Tshikona*, with the teacher teaching his students the wind-dance steps of *Tshikona* performance. Video file available at www.Cambridge.org/Muthivhi

Teacher teaching his students the steps of Tshikona, while. Video 5 illustrates community performance of Tshikona.

Therefore, Tshikona has close association with ceremonial occasions regarding the celebration of the first fruits and the coming of the first rains during the planting seasons. Meanwhile, the appearance of these migratory birds was viewed as signifying nature's providence and was celebrated by the institution of the communal *thevhula* event, involving which involved the throwing of beer to the ground as thanksgiving to ancestor gods accompanied by the tshikona of thevhula. Tshikona, therefore, plays a central role in the celebratory activities signifying the highest authorisation of the events within communal structures, as well as signifying solidarity and common purpose (see Blacking, 1995b, 1970; Nemapate, 2010; Schutte, 1978; Stayt, 1931). The abstract steps of tshikona represent significant historical events, important historical personalities, values and customs, including the values imbued on the behaviour of the storks. Meanwhile, in African tradition, are associated with qualities related to statecraft such as diplomacy and wisdom. For example, the Horus Falcon was one of such symbols, as well as the *Luvhimba* Falcon in the *Njelele* and Great Zimbabwe traditions (Beach, 1998; Ralushai, 1978; Ralushai and Gray, 1977; Robins, 2000).

Therefore, tshikona performance is revealed in its association with qualities attributed to white-bellied Abdim's storks. Consequently, tshikona is, therefore, revealed in its mutual embodiment with natural and cultural processes, an

Figure 6 A whole village performance of *Tshikona*, made up of young and old members of community. Video file available at www.Cambridge.org/Muthivhi

unbroken continuum never to be rendered dichotomous; separate and oppositional. That is, the communal values of white-bellied storks are subsumed into the culturally situated community practices embedded in the activities of tshikona performance. This cultural embodiment of knowledge is further revealed in contemporary research findings. For example, recent research findings on animal behaviour support the view in their communal and social organisation, storks socialise their storklings in communal flying as a muster, but such communal orientation to socialisation produces capabilities for flying independently. That is, according to these findings, within the social migration preference by storks, their young gain experience of flying in the context of social groups but, at the same time, it is through this social group context that their young gain the independence to ignore social influences (Avolio et al., 2024).

Tshikona therefore celebrates communal values which it embodies both in its organisation and in its performance. The abstract steps represent many of the communal horticultural activities such as planting seeds, gathering peanuts, and baboons stealing mealies. The steps also represent significant events or embody the actions of important historical figures. However, in its anticlockwise movement, tshikona, like all other performances discussed above, embodies the direction, and the circularities, of the south-easterly trade winds which are critical for precipitation, especially in north-eastern South Africa, including East Africa. The pre-colonial weather forecasting traditions in the north-eastern part of South Africa was reported in ethnographic literature. Such knowledge, involving atmospheric patterns, was undoubtedly based on ingenious meteorological observation skills such as the direction and speed of the south-easterly trade winds, as well as the associated climatic and atmospheric conditions (see Schutte, 1978; Stayt, 1931).

Tshikona, evidently, embodies cycles of the seasons, with the spring beginning as the seasons of plenty in which the thevhula thanksgiving is performed, at the same time that the storks and the trade winds, as mutually embedded processes of nature, are celebrated, with this mutual embedding of processes manifest in, and through, tshikona performance itself. This culturally situated knowledge practices are, therefore, enacted as embodied knowledge instantiating students' practical actions and personal experiences. The enactment of embodied knowledge practices can therefore become the grounding principle with regard to the creation of a pedagogy that supersedes the epistemological approaches that underpin contemporary post-apartheid pedagogy in South Africa. That is, such a decolonising approach to pedagogy can begin with the moral assumption that all students have knowledge and skills, and are capable of learning and succeeding in their learning, provided that teachers and other relevant stakeholders commit to the creation of conditions necessary for such success to be realised.

Therefore, embodied knowledge as the axiomatic grounding of pedagogy, prioritises an ethical dimension of knowledge, to do with social justice and equity, thereby addressing issues of culturalhistorical relevance and sociopolitical contingencies. The ethical grounding of knowledge supersedes the confining epistemological criteria that characterise traditional models of pedagogy, by grounding pedagogy on ideals of open-ended, whole inquiry approach that does not render knowledge dichotomous vis-à-vis their practical pursuit of knowledge, personal goals, interests, and emotions. In this postulation, concepts are revealed in their process of transformation and are, consequently, not rendered reified – that is, frozen in time.

Therefore, from the perspective of the 'whole inquiry process', knowledge is taken to be open-ended and indeterminate, as well as culturally situated, historically contingent, and practically relevant. At the same time, knowledge is understood to be inherently social, politically and ideologically saturated, and, ultimately, ethically responsible. As a result, knowledge reveals particular historical-political struggles taking place in society and within schooling. These struggles, for the majority of South Africa's teachers and their students, including, of course, communities at large, is waged in the context of classroom teaching and learning, including on the peripheries of extracurricular activities where the culturally situated knowledge practices and traditions, including African languages, are enacted despite the continued exclusionary practices manifested in, and through, the coercive and hegemonic epistemologies that guide contemporary post-apartheid pedagogy.

Figure 7, therefore, demonstrates an instance wherein teachers could create learning events from their students' embodied culturally situated knowledge practices, transforming their embodied knowledge through its enactment as performatory approach to pedagogy into tools for self-learning and identity development, thereby revealing knowledge and concepts as whole inquiry process. In this ethical grounding of pedagogy on values of agentic contribution to collective social transformation and self-identity, knowledge is posited as having no predetermined linear structure, no rigid prediction of next stages and end goals. That is, knowledge is understood as a whole dynamic process of mutually embedded, interdependent, intertwined, and mutually implicating elements, embodying the past in the present – out of which future possibilities are created.

Therefore, like a ceaseless stream, and the river into which it pours, such as represented in Figure 7, with the river Nile meandering down from its catchment areas and tributaries in the east African subcontinent, starting in the Ugandan and Ethiopian highlands, curving down South Sudan and the Sudan to the Egyptian desert plains on its way to the Mediterranean Sea. Indeed, that body of water does not cease as it is transformed into ocean currents, indelibly intertwined with the trade winds and the resultant precipitation, here illustrated by the south-easterly trade winds responsible for the weather phenomena and precipitation in northern South Africa and the east African coastal areas. Consequently, the entire process implicates the epistemic questions such as involved in the physics of the earth's magnetic field and the anticlockwise direction of the trade winds, as well as the natural behaviour of Abdim's storks, the climatic conditions and the weather phenomena of these specific areas – all profoundly interconnected with cultural processes involved in the tshikona anticlockwise movement and the implicantions of mutual embeddedness of the natural and cultural processes, including the associated mutual entailments of these processes in bodily perception of concepts, apprehended in, and through, their process of transformation. The culturally situated performance traditions therefore reveal profound interconnectedness of natural and cultural processes, and the embodiment of knowledge about natural phenomena within processes of culture, such as embedded in tshikona performance. This embodied knowledge is consequently transformed through the performatory ontoepistemology into practical concepts which, inevitably, are perceived as meaningful tools for personal pursuit of self-knowledge, social transformation, and, simultaneously, identity development.

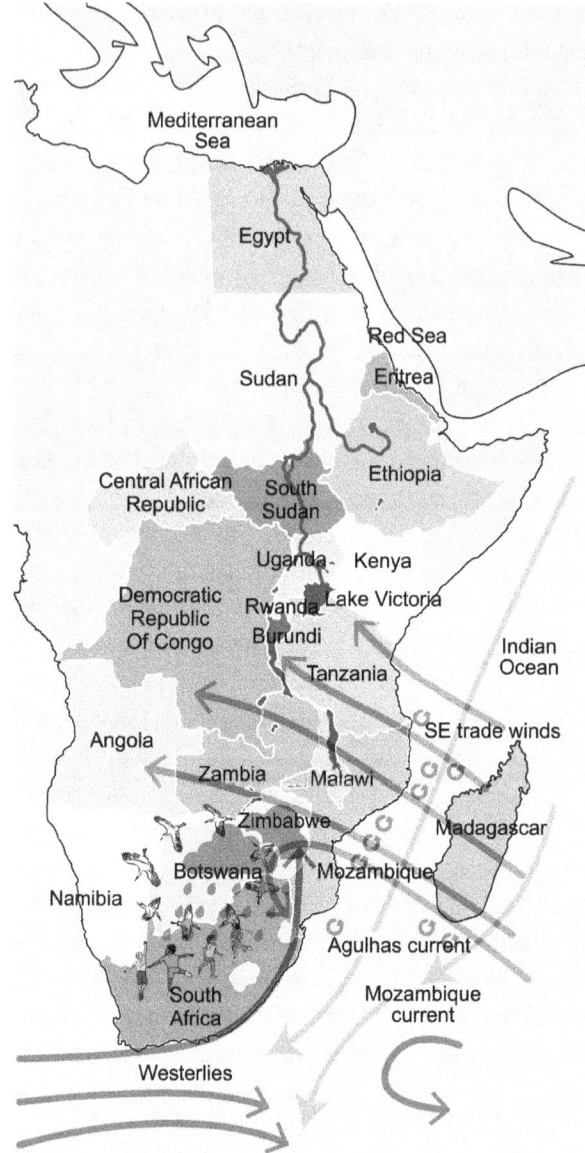

Figure 7 *Whole process inquiry* approach to pedagogy

4.5 Heritage and Historical Studies

The thematic approach to knowledge is particularly relevant for heritage and historical studies, subject areas that have always been troubled within the South African schooling system, including within the contemporary post-apartheid pedagogy. The demarcation of knowledge into normative subject disciplines has especially worsened the situation. The action was undoubtedly informed by the political ideologies associated with neocolonial projects and the associated neoliberal agendas. History, in particular, has always been politically charged and ideologically prejudiced, premised on objectivist and adaptationist methodologies that espouse hegemonic and exclusionary criteria for validity and legitimacy.

This prescribed model of pedagogy, premised on objectivist ontology, espouses abstract and mentalist methodologies that eschew culturally situated community practices, identity development, and the thematic approach to learning and development. In this approach, knowledge is validated from the point of view of its epistemic grounding, to do with questions of rationality and truth value. This approach is unfortunately pursued in complete exclusion of the ethical grounding of knowledge, to do with questions of social justice and equity.

The dilemma facing post-apartheid pedagogy today, relative to the conundrum involving the organisation of the content and methodology of the subject discipline of history, is discussed in the more recent publication by Muller and Young (2019). In this discussion, Muller and Young (2019) acknowledge the dilemma facing the prescription of what they call powerful knowledge, in regard to school history subject discipline. The authors distinguish between approaches that draw from their own notion of 'powerful knowledge', which underpins the prescription for content knowledge and methodology of history subject matter. These criteria for validating and legitimising knowledge in the discipline of history, according to the first strand in the application of the concept of powerful knowledge, have offered what is deemed to be a more objectivist and cognitivist interpretation. This approach is premised on such objectivist and cognitivist conceptualisations that apprehends knowledge as 'substantive and inherent to the subject discipline' – the notions of 'historical facts', the 'hinterland of the discipline', history's 'distinctive pursuit of truth', 'how valid claims can be made', what constitutes evidence for a claim', 'quality of argumentation', 'judgement making, and 'fidelity to evidence' (Muller and Young, 2019, pp. 11–12).

This list of ideologically imbued categorical terms, posited as defining objective criteria and universal norms on the basis of which knowledge can be determined once and for all, is all too familiar to many of us who studied school history within neocolonial classrooms. It is certainly a coercive and hegemonic postulation that jettisons subjectivity, agency, creativity, innovation, and identity development. Knowledge of history is thus fashioned in ways that are exclusionary of non-dominant, non-Western knowledge traditions, including the non-dualist and, especially, critical-theoretic and emancipatory methodologies and approaches. In positing the second strand in the interpretation of the epistemological grounding of the concept of 'powerful knowledge', positing a view of knowledge and pedagogy devoid of context and human subjectivity, Muller and Young (2019) argue that according to this interpretation, the impact of external circumstances and interests, as well as the everyday world of politics and daily life, 'supervenes'. The dualistc notion of external interests and circumstances supervening in the process of content selection is, unfortunately, postulated in the solipsistic, mentalist, and mechanical sense where processes are taken to unfold on their own and never subject to human purposive and agentive actions.

Therefore, external influences are rendered as impacting on internal structures and procedures of the disciplinary knowledge processes by some mechanical means, and teachers and their students are positioned as passive and without agency. In this half-hearted acceptance of the practical reality of context and its inevitable influences on normative standards, the laws of the physical sciences are transposed to those postulated for the discipline of history. That is, powerful knowledge, as regards the discipline of history, functions by emulating the standards of the physical sciences. Both subject disciplines are posited as united in 'their distinctive pursuit of truth'; conceptualised in terms of abstract concepts, and 'the progressive deepening of the respective subject areas' distinctive disciplinary forms of reasoning'. Therefore, physics knowledge structure is viewed as distinguished by what is termed, 'within-topic progression and cumulation' of concepts, hierarchical and vertical structure of knowledge and hence, conceptual ladder to climb, or conceptual depth progression. On the contrary, the discipline of history is distinguished by horizontal knowledge structure—with no conceptual ladder to climb, progressing by developing new languages and posing new problems and therefore tending towards narrative accounts and argumentation. That is, history grows by way of 'progressive deepening of the ramifications of the entailment of causal argument—a deepening of the appreciation of the 'network of "if ... then" reasoning' ... that sits behind the claims advanced' (Muller and Young, 2019, p. 12).

The implication for such rendering of history pedagogics is that both – in the selection of knowledge and related methodologies, as well as in the actual practices of classroom teaching and learning – subjectivity, including the associated processes of agency, creativity, and innovation, are virtually eliminated. What is prioritised is the confining criteria of the subject discipline and its rendering of knowledge and pedagogy into contemplative and mentalist endeavours that only relate to subjectivity and context by chance, and never the result of wilful acts, answerable deeds, and purposeful pursuit of knowledge and self-identity development. The pathway to connecting knowledge and pedagogy to identity development and students' culturally situated community practices and knowledge traditions can be understood as embedded in the methodological propositions. As a result, the knowledge is purged of human subjectivity and identity in the quest for the normativity of methodologies that prescribe history as the 'pursuit of truth', confined to 'what passes for an argument', 'historical facts' that make up 'substantive knowledge', and 'the substrate of the past', conceptualised – essentially, as the solipsistic pursuit of 'the hinterland of the discipline' (Muller and Young, 2019, p. 11).

As a consequence, the thematic approach is virtually eradicated on grounds that it lacks disciplinary rigor and, hence, leading to superficial acquisition of the horizons of the discipline. For example, in arguing against the thematic approach to history pedagogy on the criteria of discipline-based, powerful knowledge methodology, Kallaway (2012) maintains that historical content needs to be 'defended in terms of the *criteria of discipline-based knowledge* in the profession of history and in terms of their pedagogic suitability/teachability for teenagers' (Kallaway, 2012, p. 57, emphasis in the original). Further, in lamenting a policy directive for the inclusion of the thematic approach within contemporary post-apartheid pedagogy, where, in practice, such would be deemed to be relevant and necessary, the criticism has been that such an approach would only produce superficiality and would thus undermine the credibility of the discipline.

It is unfortunate, therefore, from the point of view of decolonising approach, that the denial of the thematic approach to teaching history inevitably undermines connecting pedagogy to students' culturally situated community practices and knowledge traditions and hence, agentic contribution to collective communal practices and identity development. As a result, the contribution of students non-dominant, non-Western communities are, unfortunately, denied the opportunity to connect knowledge products in the subject discipline to their subjective senses, and the opportunity for meaningful pursuit of knowledge authentically connected to students' interests, goals, and identity development. Consequently, the history of Western conquest is conveniently presented as the dominant approach, with the resultant subordinate position of non-dominant communities, including their students' struggles with the objectified knowledge rendered logical consequence of the historical development of societies.

In South African pedagogy, history began with the Western settlement of the Cape of Good Hope in 1652, proceeding to the systematic conquest of the hinterland, a civilising process often justified by the ostensibly higher levels of socioeconomic development of South Africa in comparison to many of their African counterparts. Western civilisation is therefore presented as the end goal of the process of human historical development, with Western epistemologies similarly serving as the benchmark of what is valid and legitimate. On this basis, the exclusion of pre-colonial African civilisations, such as the thirteenth-century Mapungubwe civilisation in the Limpopo River valley, a UNESCO heritage site in the northern part of South Africa, and its association with the subsequent great Zimbabwe civilisation (Beach, 1998; Liesegang, 1977; Loubser, 1989), was deemed not valid historical content which could legitimately be studied through methods that thematically connect pedagogy to agency and identity.

At the same time, the contemporary post-apartheid pedagogy, espousing epistemological methodologies and the dichotomous approach to knowledge jettisons the thematic exploration of African historical development in faviour of the Westerncentric cannons and their exclusionary methodologies that prescribe objectivity and neutrality. That is, the history of Africa, and it entailment in the Nilotic civilisations, for example, and undoubtedly manifests in, and through, the natural and cultural processes pervasive in the continent, and – for example, in the physical and geological features of the Nile river itself, perceived in the interconnectedness of the natural and cultural processes. Meanwhile, the various cultural practices and linguistic traditions are left unexplored and never imagined in their implications, such as pertaining to Africa's lanner falcon tradition. The lanner falcon tradition manifestly spans such vast expanse as the ancient Egyptian Horus Falcon, the *Njelele* falcon on the Limpopo river valley in northern South Africa and southern Zimbabwe, as well as the Great Zimbabwe falcon, all providing a potential unitary view and the associated implications as regards the historical knowledge, epitomising common qualities attributed to natural processes, vis-à-vis their ontoepistemic implications for culturalhistorical processes (Beach, 1998; Ralushai, 1978; Ralushai and Gray, 1977; Robins, 2000).

4.6 Conclusion

Therefore, the decolonising approach to pedagogy grounded on ethical questions begins with the postulation of knowledge as embedded in the procedures by which it is realised, embodied by students through their culturally situated community practices and knowledge traditions which they enact as an agentic contribution to their self-learning and development. That is, knowledge and concepts are realised by students as practical activities unfolding in real-life conditions, and practical circumstances, enacted as it is transformed into new concepts for self-learning and development.

As a result, the decolonising approach to pedagogy demands that teachers, rather than adopting a purely epistemic and contemplative posture to knowledge and learning, perceive their students as knowledgeable and capable of conceptual understanding to be revealed in, and through, their meaningful enactment of, and agentive contribution to, collective social transformation. Students come to learn and acquire moral values and attitudes for social contribution, thereby making a difference in their community at the same time that they acquire practical concepts and skills. This is an ethically grounded approach to pedagogy that – nonetheless, does not abandon the epistemic criteria but rather supersedes them by subsuming them under a more developed ethically grounded form of knowledge, knowing, and being, espousing the vision of a future predicated on values of social justice and equity.

The epistemic, therefore, is subsumed under an ethically grounded knowledge postulation geared at promoting the moral vision of profound human interconnectedness, vis-à-vis other humans. Therefore, the ethical grounding of pedagogy undoubtedly privileges ideals of solidarity and collaboration, including answerable deeds of responsibility, accountability, and care, for, and towards social others. Such an utopian view of agentic contribution to collective community practices and self-identity development, embodied in culturally situated community practices and knowledge traditions, is evidently contradictory to the vision espoused through, and implicated in, contemporary post-apartheid pedagogy and its underlying epistemologies espousing pernicious individualism, as well as a palpable lack of empathy and care, including a sense of responsibility and accountability.

5 Ethical and Political Grounding of Knowledge and Pedagogy

In prescribing exclusionary criteria for what counts as valid knowledge that prepares students for the demands of life in dominant socio-economic system, contemporary post-apartheid pedagogy and its underlying epistemologies make several fundamental errors about learning, knowledge acquisition, and human development, including the moral grounding of pedagogy in general. The 'power' of knowledge, including school knowledge, can reasonably not be prescribed to reside exclusively in concepts posited as devoid of subjectivity and context. Moral values and ethical dimension cannot be completely and wholly purged from knowledge pursuit so as to render knowledge in accordance with the epistemic criteria of neutrality and objectivity (Stetsenko, 2023). On the contrary, from the decolonising pedagogy standpoint, practical everyday concerns, including the real-life strivings and struggles to which humans are positioned, should comprise of their ethical grounding of knowledge and pedagogy.

That is, from the current critical-theoretic and ethically grounded approach to knowledge and pedagogy, human subjectivity, interests, goals, purposes, and emotions comprise the very core and essence of what knowledge and pedagogy are made of. This is a stance that repudiates the normativity and orthodoxy that underpin accounts of knowledge, and hence pedagogy, as geared towards revealing the world as it is. That is, in order to decolonise knowledge, and pedagogy, we must first and foremost, debunk the myths of knowledge – including physics – as geared towards the uncovering of truths and reality as purged from ourselves, including the associated beliefs in the objectivity of 'raw facts' and 'pristine reality', construed as devoid of, and separate from, human experiences, emotions, goals, and purposes.

Further, to debunk the myths of objectivist epistemologies, which posit knowledge and pedagogy along the lines of objectivist model of science positing a view of science as geared towards the understanding the world as 'it is', and the social sciences (including the humanities) as following behind in the quest for an objective world devoid of human subjectivity and divorced from human goals and purposes, we need to debunk such mythologies by exposing their foundations in Western coercive and hegemonic epistemologies and the associated political ideologies. These hegemonic and exclusionary epistemologies are revealed in their prescriptions of confining parameters for what counts as valid and legitimate knowledge and hence, pedagogy. Consequently, the postulation of 'powerful knowledge', separate from and oppositional to everyday forms of knowledge is revealed as a political ideology that disguises historical inequalities for inevitable consequences of the natural order of things. According to this ideology of adaptation to the status quo of domination and control, the approach avoids the analysis of historical and political processes, rendering historical and politically contingencies – in the logic of colonial ethnocentric epistemologies, – into natural inevitabilities, and the logical consequence of how things are in the world. At the same time, the normative value embodied by knowledge and concepts posited as abstract and contemplative are denied, while concepts are posited as progressing by laws of nature, only revealed with and accessible to the priviledged social class, mostly from dominant sociopolitical status.

This is the normative tradition in which the ideology of 'powerful' knowledge', including the notion of 'specialised' knowledge and concepts, has been formulated and infused to comprise of the structure of contemporary post-apartheid pedagogy. However, the application of this epistemological criteria into the contemporary post-apartheid pedagogy has not been without contradictions, as can be seen with the contentious and politically charged topic involving connecting pedagogy to students' identity development, including the associated subject regarding the thematic approach to knowledge.

Therefore, in countering and debunking prevailing coercive colonial epistemologies and the associated political ideology of adaptation to the status quo of passivity and objectivity, the current approach to decolonising pedagogy espouses the ethos of contribution, transformation, including the philosophical centrality of activism. That is, the decolonising approach to pedagogy postulates an ethical grounding of knowledge, espousing the ideals of social justice and equity. As a result, the decolonising approach to pedagogy challenges Western orthodoxies and their solipsistic methodologies that render students' culturally situated and embodied knowledge practices invalid, thus denying students their inherent capacities for meaningful pursuit of knowledge, and the agentic contribution to collective practices, including identity development.

5.1 Transformative Agency and Identity Development

Therefore, as opposed to neoliberal notions of agency and identity that prioritises division and separation of people on the basis of their race and ethnic categories, and so on, with the consequent tragedy of the colonial and apartheid legacies, the notion of agency and identity postulated in the decolonising approach to pedagogy herein proposed take a fundamentally different form. For example, Engeström et al. (2014) explain that transformative agency differs from neoliberal interpretation because it goes beyond individual action to prioritise social transformation. That is, transformative agency arises from contradictions, emerging from life's strivings and struggles, and evolving over prolonged periods of time. This agentic condition, according to this position, goes beyond the 'situational here-and-now by explicating and envisioning new possibilities for collective change efforts' (Engeström et al., 2014, p. 124).

In expanding on this concept Stetsenko (2020) argues that the concept of transformative agency overcomes traditional dichotomies that characterise agency as exclusively associated with individuals on the one hand, and the social as devoid of individual contribution on the other hand. In this view, transformative agency is premised on collaborative social practices as involving people acting and doing things together, while simultaneously creating their life through answerable deeds, life quests, and meaningful pursuits enacted as collective efforts and struggles for a sought-after-future. This approach therefore jettisons mentalist and contemplative approaches that deny inherent human creativity and innovation. In positing an approach that focuses on agentic contributions to collective social practices as a new form of life, transformative agency prioritises the ontological primacy of answerable deeds, as the axiological grounding of being human, as well as the profound interconnectedness that constitutes the deepest attribute and basic characteristic of human life (see Stetsenko, 2020a, 2007).

The decolonising approach to pedagogy, therefore, premised on the postulation of transformative agency, has fundamental implications for contemporary post-apartheid pedagogy. The passivity of the normativity and orthodoxy that position teachers and students as unproductive, rendering their classroom activities into meaningless, mechanical processes of fitting in and coping with the prescribed models and predetermined methodologies is superseded by the ethos of agentic contribution to community practices, grounded on culturally situated knowledge practices which are embodied by students and enacted as meaningful pursuit of self-knowledge and identity development.

As a result, the thematic approach to knowledge ensures that pedagogy is connected authentically and meaningfully with students' culturally situated community practices and knowledge traditions. That is, students transform their embodied knowledge and concepts into practical-theoretic tools, whereby they acquire grounded conceptual understanding that is revealed to them in and through the course of their practical engagements with reality. In this postulation, teachers commit to creating opportunities for their students, for them to enact their embodied knowledge, and thereby perceive concepts in their process of transformation and therefore not in their stating and reified form.

At the same time, the idea of transformative agency is inextricably connected with the related idea of identity development. Identity, unfortunately, has had an unfortunate legacy in the turmoils of the history of South Africa. In this history the notion of identity was entangled with the apartheid ideology of segregation and racial supremacy. In contrast to this dichotomous postulation of identity development, identity development in the present approach is taken to be grounded on the unfolding of the self-, as an activist recreation of cultural tools for meaningful self-development and hence, profound interconnectedness of selfhood unfolding in, and through, collective social practices. Viana and Stetsenko (2011) propose a perspective that links identity development to students' 'forward-looking', activist practices of social transformation whereby agentic contribution is made possible by students' own active recreation of cultural tools vis-à-vis their potential application in future practices 'as tools of meaningful quest and, therefore, identity' (Viana and Stetsenko, 2011, p. 320).

Identity development, therefore, is not taken to be merely an outcome of teaching and learning but the very substance and fabric of pedagogic engagement, as well as the vehicle through which pedagogy is realised. According to this view, knowledge is transformed – both by teachers and by their students – into tools for social transformation and self-realisation, as well as a tool for meaningful pursuit of self-knowledge, including identity development (Viana and Stetsenko, 2011). Therefore, according to this view, a pedagogy grounded on ethos of agentive contribution to social transformation and identity development demands that teachers and their students take charge of the practices of teaching and learning and ground these on their culturally situated community practices and knowledge traditions, as an ethico-political grounding of knowledge and pedagogy unfolding in, and revealed through, such grounding as identity development and self-realisation.

This decolonising approach to pedagogy, therefore, deconstructs the colonial and apartheid ontology – and their ensuing epistemologies of racial and ethnic, including the tribal divisions that continue to be deeply entrenched, even representing something of a ticking time bond for the contemporary post-apartheid society and schooling. The traditional dichotomised language identities, the socio-economic class divisions of school identities, with their consequent racialised performance outcomes, still very much predicated on age-old colonial foundations, including the associated conundrum of linguistic divisions, continue to undergird the racialised and hierarchical performance processes.

5.2 Embodied Knowledge and Performatory Pedagogy

In the decolonising approach to pedagogy herein proposed, knowledge is posited as embodied by the students, and they enact this knowledge in, and through, their culturally situated knowledge practices. That is, students learn from their culture and society and acquire the knowledge and skills connected to practices in their culture, practices which are relevant and significant to the students and their communities, therefore providing ethical grounding for students' practical, real-life condition of being children growing up into the norms and values of their society and culture.

In an approach that resonates with the idea of embodied knowledge enactment and hence, the performatory pedagogy approach herein proposed, is what Holzman (1997) has called non-epistemological performatory pedagogy. According to this view, performatory pedagogy creates a non-epistemological learning environment conducive for doing or enacting performance. This is in opposition to the epistemological paradigm that prioritises truth and objectivity, thereby stifling creativity and innovation on the part of teachers and their students. At the same time, performatory approach to pedagogy supersedes disciplinary prescriptions of artificial boundaries between sociocultural and educational contexts, including the associated hierarchical positioning of teachers vis-à-vis their students, as well as the dichotomous postulation of school knowledge vis-à-vis everyday forms of knowledge. Performative, or performatory pedagogy creates collaborative learning, removing the hierarchical structure of knowledge and pedagogy in favour of participatory, collaborative, and dialogic approaches.

One of the performatory pedagogy approach Holzman (1997) reports is the South Bronx elementary school in New York City piloted in 1996. In this performatory approach, which unfolded as an intervention programme in regard to what the local board of directors had deemed to be poor student attendance and academic performance, the performative approach focused on assisting the Grades 1 to 6 students to create something positive in and out of their lives using improvisation games, creating comedy sketches using themes from their lives to enact them as public performance at the end of school year. As such, students had the opportunity to make decisions about how the play should be like, when they wanted to perform, taking full responsibility for their own actions and their performance. Consequently, students performed the roles of their own choosing, recreating the roles which they may have played in their real-life situations and creating themes in which they would want to see themselves playing such roles and thereby perceiving themselves and their peers in these roles, as capable and successful students. The students also began to perceive themselves as attending to their responsibilities, as well as accountable for each other, thereby also learning the values of collaboration and agentic contribution, including creating a new environment of their schooling in which they transform themselves into successful learners who attend to their responsibilities.

Contemporary post-apartheid pedagogy unfortunately remains under the grip of disciplinary epistemological postulation, where emphasis is placed on success conceived as solipsistic and mentalist rendering of literacy acquisition, number operations, and the acquisition of objectified knowledge and scientific concepts. Teachers feel enormously overwhelmed by the requirements to teach objectified knowledge and reified concepts, connecting these concepts artificially for their students, to 'read with meaning', as well as do mathematics, all in the manner of mechanically connecting commodified subject matter knowledge and the reified concepts to students' subjective experiences and personal sense, including their interests, and goals. An instance of a 10-year-old girl, Bele (pseudonym used), which I experienced when conducting observation of teaching and learning in a Grade 6 classroom in northern South Africa, in 2000, has relevance:

I had the pleasure to observe the young Bele in a sixth-grade classroom at a school in Sibasa during one of my research visits in the area, which is relevant for purposes of illustrating the enactment of embodied culturally situated community practices and knowledge traditions. On one of the afternoon lessons in Grade 6, taught by a male teacher who also acted as school principal, I decided to go around as usual observing what each student was writing, as the teacher had finished teaching and had given a written exercise. I moved around from one student to the other, asking them questions so I could learn from each student what they were writing about and how they understood the task. The students were generally keen to let me see their writing and they eagerly explained what it was they were writing.

However, when I come to Bele, I realised that she did not readily show me her written work like the other students but seemed to be trying to conceal her work using her elbow. She also seems to be withdrawn and introverted, unwilling to show her written work, I took it that the girl was just shy and I did not want to embarrass her by trying to ask her questions, since she had put her arm over her writing, indicating that she may not be confident about showing her work.

As I moved on, the teacher advanced towards me, pulling me aside and speaking in a hushed voice explaining to me that the student in question was a 'slow learner', and that she was struggling with school work. He further explained that the school has recommended her for specialist learning support offered by local authorities.

After I had proceeded with my observation of all the remaining students in class, and was about to leave as the bell indicating midday the break time had just gone off, Bele drew my attention to herself, calling me 'teacher', and indicating that she had wanted to tell me something. On turning and giving her my attention, Bele asked me if I had wanted her to perform a dance for me. I was amused at the request and, before I could respond, a chorus of voices from the collective of the students in class encouraged me to allow her a chance to perform for me. I acknowledged Bele's request and told her I had liked to see her perform.

The young girl stood up with pride and a sense of gratification, unlike in an earlier episode when she seemed embarrassed to show me her written work and discuss it with me. Bele immediately went to the front of class, with her peers in class cheering and encouraging her on her role. Bele started to dance a solo dance usually performed by expert solo *tshigombela* performers. Her dancing clearly showed intricate skills in elegant movement of legs and hands, including the occasional jumping and stomping with both feet, and hands thrown up and down while swirling up, down, front and back, sometimes one hand landing on her back while the other one facing the front. She performed an elegant *u losha* tribute in the end, and so confident and exquisite was the performance. I joined the whole class cheering the masterful performance.

I congratulated Bele, and also thanked her for her outstanding performance. Immediately after expressing my compliments, the teacher approached and explained that this girl was in fact the best performer and that she was also responsible for teaching other students and the teachers about traditional performances in the school. The teacher further explained to me that the girl, Bele, came from a family where traditional performances are commonly performed.

This incident remained with me as a lasting intrigue, regarding the contradictions of performance in contemporary post-apartheid schooling and pedagogy on the one hand, versus the culturally situated knowledge practices which students embody and enact, but often with no recognition and acknowledgement in the formal structure of pedagogy. Therefore, in the enactment of the embodied and culturally situated knowledge practices, much learning and competent performance unfold and is manifested. However, the contradictions involving Bele's reported 'slow learning' vis-à-vis her 'outstanding performance' and her exquisite enactment of her embodied knowledge and culturally situated community practices, remain a momentous event epitomising the inherent capacities of students, and their associated knowledge they embody and enact, but which, unfortunately, continue to lack recognition within the fixed curriculum structure of contemporary post-apartheid pedagogy.

5.3 Conclusion

Therefore, the contribution of the present monograph is in its attempt at exposing and debunking the mythology of objective knowledge and concepts – including scientific knowledge – purged from our subjectivity, value free and neutral, progressing by laws of nature and unencumbered by human endeavour. As Stetsenko (2023) has indicated, the political expediency of objectivist knowledge, including value free and neutral methodologies, have been debunked many times in critical sociocultural research, including by physical and natural scientists. The tragedy of the contemporary post-apartheid pedagogy and its underlying epistemologies, therefore, is in its dogmatic insistence on objectivity and neutrality, including the claim about raw facts, pristine reality and science as disinterested pursuit of knowledge purged from our subjectivity — a process aimed at knowing the world and reality as it is. As Brownovsky, cited in Stetsenko (2023, p. 25), has explained: 'One aim of the physical sciences has been to give an actual picture of the material world. One achievement of physics in the twentieth century has been to show that such an aim is unattainable.'

Therefore debunking the myths of objectivity and neutrality, including the associated methodologies espousing solipsism and mentalism, is important for the decolonising approach to pedagogy, since these politically expedient epistemologies underpin contemporary post-apartheid pedagogy. The triumph of Western Olympian view of history and culture is, unfortunately, cemented in the hegemonic epistemologies and their tacit insistence for non-dominant societies to follow uncritically and acquiesce to the colonial logic, with the endgoal of domination and control.

Further, as contribution to a model for decolonising pedagogy, the epistemic grounding of knowledge prioritising issues of validity, truth, and rationality is superseded by the ethical grounding, prioritising questions of morality, to do with what is correct and morally right under given circumstances, and how – given the prevailing historical and political circumstances – knowledge and pedagogy should, and 'out to' be, organised. Therefore, the decolonising approach to pedagogy is grounded on the assumption that all students are capable, and that they bring into schooling and classroom teaching and learning the rich repertoire of the enactments their culturally situated knowledge practices which they embody. Teachers recreate the learning or pedagogic events – subsuming students' intense emotional experiences – whereby students enact their embodied knowledge, transforming this knowledge into meaningful tools for their ongoing exploratory activities geared towards social transformation and self-development.

References

Arievitch, I. M., & Stetsenko, A. (2000). The quality of cultural tools and cognitive development: Gal'perin's perspective and its implications. *Human Development*, 43(2), 69–92. https://doi.org/10.1159/000022661.

Apple, M. W. (2001). Comparing Neo-liberal projects and inequality in education. *Comparative Education*, 37(4), 409–423. https://doi.org/10.1080/03050060120091229.

Appadurai, A. (2001). The globalization of archaeology and heritage: A discussion with Arjun.

Appadurai. *Journal of Social Archaeology* 1(1), 35–49. https://doi.org/10.1177/146960530100100103.

Avolio, C., Flack, A., & Bronnvik, H. (2024). Storks fly with a little help from their friends: Young animals in particular prefer to move with their conspecifics. *Max Planck Institute of Animal Behaviour*, www.mpg.de/21823848/0412-ornr-storks-fly-with-a-little-help-from-their-friends-987453-x.

Bakhtin, M. M. (1993). Towards a Philosophy of the Act. In V. Liapunov, & M. Holquist, eds., Austin: University of Texas, 1–132. https://doi.org/10.7560/765344.

Beach, D. (1998). Cognitive archaeology and imaginary history at Great Zimbabwe. *Current Anthropology*, 10(1), 47–72. https://doi.org/10.1086/204698.

Bernstein, B. (2000) *Pedagogy, Symbolic Control and Identity: Theory, Research, Critique*, 2nd ed. Oxford: Rowman & Littlefield.

Blacking, J. (1970). Tonal organisation of the music of two Venda initiation schools. *Ethnomusicology*, 4(1), 1–56. https://doi.org/10.2307/850292.

Blacking, J. (1995a). Music, culture, & experience. In R. Byron, ed., *Selected Papers of John Blacking*. Chicago: The University of Chicago Press.

Blacking, J. (2007). Songs, dances, mimes and symbolism of Venda girls' initiation schools: Part 2: Milayo. African Studies, https://doi.org/10.1080/00020186908707306.

Blacking, J. (1995b). *Venda Children's Songs: A Study in Ethnomusicological Analysis*, Chicago: The University of Chicago Press.

Blacking, J. (1971). *Yearbook of the International Folk Music Council*, (3). Cambridge: Cambridge University Press, 91–108.

Cole, M. (1996). *Cultural Psychology: A Once and Future Discipline*. Cambridge, MA: Harvard University Press.

Department of Education. (1996). *Curriculum Framework for General and Further Education and Training*. Pretoria: National Department of Education.

Department of Education. (2002). *Revised National Curriculum Statement: Grades R-9 (Schools) Policy Languages*. Home Language. Pretoria: Government Printer.

Department of Education. (2009). *Report of the Task Team on the Review of the Implementation of the National Curriculum Statement: Final Report, October 2009*. Pretoria: South Africa.

Department of Education. (1997). *Outcomes-Based Education in South Africa: Background information for Educators*. Pretoria: National Department of Education.

Engeström, Y., Sannino, A., & Virkkunen, J. (2014). On the methodological demands of formative interventions. *Mind, Culture, and Activity*, 21(2), 118–128. https://doi.org/10.1080/10749039.2014.891868.

Enslin, P., & Hedge, N., (2023). Decolonizing higher education: The university in the new age of Empire. *Journal of Philosophy of Education*, 58(2–3), 227–241. https://doi.org/10.1093/jopedu/qhad052.

Forster, D. F. (2010). A generous ontology: Identity as a process of intersubjective discovery. An African theological contribution, *HTS Toelogiese/Theological Studies*, 66(1), 731–812. https://doi.org/10.4102/hts.v66i1.731.

Gould, S. J. (1996). *The Mismeasure of Man*. New York: W. W. Norton.

Griffiths, D. (2019). #FeesMustfall and the decolonized university in South Africa: Tensions and opportunities in a globalising world. *International Journal of Educational Research*, 94, 143–149. https://doi.org/10.1016/j.ijer.2019.01.004.

Hardman, J. (2024). Decolonising pedagogy: A critical engagement with debates in the university in South Africa. *Journal of Education*, 94, 146–160. https://doi.org/10.17159/2520-9868/i94a09.

Holzman, L. (1997). *Schools for Growth: Radical Alternatives to Current Educational Models*. London: Lawrence Erlbaum Associates.

Jansen, J. (2019). On the politics of decolonization: Knowledge, authority, and the settled curriculum, In J. Jansen, ed., *Decolonization in Universities: The Politics of Knowledge*. Johannesburg: Wits University Press, pp. 50–73.

Jansen, J. (2017). As by Fire: The End of the South African University. *Journal of Student Affairs in Africa*, 6(2), 8, 131–113. https://doi.org/10.24085/jsaa.v6i2.3316.

Jansen, J. D. (1999). Why outcomes-based education will fail: An elaboration. In J. Jansen & P. Christie, eds., *Changing Curriculum: Studies on Outcomes Based Education in South Africa*, 145–156. Cape Town: Juta.

Josep, M., Ramani, E., Tlwowane, M., & Mashatole, A. (2014). Masekitlana remembered: A performance-based ethnography of South African black children's pretend play. *South African Journal of Childhood Education*, 14(1), 1–15. https://doi.org/10.4102/sajce.v4i1.55.

Kallaway, P. (2012). History in senior secondary school CAPS 2012 and beyond: A comment, *Yesterday and Today*: Online version, www.scielo.org.za/scielo.php?script=sci_arttext&pid=S2223-03862012000100003.

Liesegang, G. (1977). New light on Venda traditions: Mahumane's account of 1730. *History in Africa*, 4, 163–181. https://doi.org/10.2307/3171583.

Loubser, J. H. N. (1989). Archaeology and early Venda history. *South African Archaeological Society*, 6, 54–61.

Loughland, T., & Sriprakash, A. (2016). Bernstein revisited: The recontextualization of equity in contemporary Australian school education. *British Journal of Sociology of Education*, 37(2), 230–247. https://doi.org/10.1080/01425692.2014.916604.

Matusov, E. (2011). Imagining No-Child-Left-Behind freed from neoliberal hijackers. *Democracy and Education*, 19(2), 1–8. https://democracyeducationjournal.org/home/vol19/iss2/2.

Matusov, E. (2008). Applying a sociocultural approach to Vygotskian academia: 'Our Tsar isn't like yours, and yours isn't like ours'. *Culture Psychology*, 14(1), 5–35. https://doi.org/10.1177/1354067X07085808.

Mbebe, A. (2016). Decolonizing the university: New directions. *Arts and Humanities in Higher Education*, 15, 29–45. https://doi.org/10.1177/1474022215618.

Miller, R. (1984). *Reflections of Mind and Culture: Inaugural Lecture*. Durban: University of Natal Press.

Moll, I. (1995). Cultural people and cultural contexts: Comments on Cole (1995) and Wertsch (1995). *Culture & Psychology*, 1(3), 361–371. https://doi.org/10.1177/1354067X9513003.

Muller, J., & Young, M. (2019): Knowledge, power and powerful knowledge re-visited. *The Curriculum Journal*, 30(2), 196–214. https://doi.org/10.1080/09585176.2019.1570292.

Muthivhi. (2014). Cultural-historical basis of literacy practices in TshiVenda-speaking South Africa's primary classrooms. *Outlines: Critical Practice Studies*, 3, 79–96. https://doi.org/10.7146/ocps.v15i3.19862.

Muthivhi, A. E. (2021). Knowledge as a tool for identity development and social transformation: A case of a teacher's activist transformative pedagogy in post-apartheid South Africa's schooling. *Outlines: Critical Practice Studies*, 22, 181–219. https://doi.org/10.7146/ocps.v22i1.121444.

Muthivhi, A. (2008). Language policy, classroom practice and concept learning in a grade one Tshivenda classroom. *Southern African Review of Education*, 14(3), 23–35.

Muthivhi, A. (2010). Ploughing new fields of knowledge: Culture and the role of community schooling in Venda. *Journal of Education*, 48, 137–153.

Nemapate, M. A. (2010). A study of structure, meaning and performance in Tshivenda traditional songs. *Unpublished Masters Dissertation*. Polokwane: University of Limpopo.

Nieuwoudt, S., Elizabeth, K., Coetzee, D. C., Engelbrecht, L., & Terblanche, E. (2019). Age- and education-related effects on cognitive functioning in Coloured South African women. *Aging, Neuropsychology, and Cognition: A Journal on Normal and Dysfunctional Development*, 27(3), 321–337. https://doi.org/10.1080/13825585.2019.1598538.

Ralushai, N. M. N. (1978). Further traditions concerning Luvhimbi and Mbedzi. *Rhodesian History*, 9, 1–12.

Ralushai, N. M. N., & Gray, J. R. (1977). Ruins and traditions of the Ngona and the Mbedzi among the Venda of the northern Transvaal. *Rhodesian History*, 8, 1–11.

Robins, G. (2000). *The Art of Ancient Egypt*. Cambridge, MA: Harvard University Press.

Schutte, A. G. (1978). Mwali in Venda: Some observations on the High God in Venda history. *Journal of Religion in Africa*, 9(2), 109–122.

Stayt, H. A. (1931). *The Bavenda*. London: Oxford University Press.

Stetsenko, A. (2007). Being-through-doing: Bakhtin and Vygotsky in dialogue. *Cultural Studies in Science Education*, 2, 746–786.

Stetsenko, A. (2020b). Critical challenges in cultural-historical activity theory: The Urgency of agency. *Cultural-Historical Psychology*, 16(2), 5–18. https://doi.org/10.17759/chp.2020160202.

Stetsenko, A. (2019a). Hope, political imagination, and agency in Marxism and beyond: Explicating the transformative worldview and ethico-ontoepistemology. *Educational Philosophy and Theory*, 52(1), 1–12. https://doi.org/10.1080/00131857.2019.1654373.

Stetsenko, A. (2023). Knowledge production as a process of making mis/takes, at the edge of uncertainty: Research as an activist, risky, and personal quest. In P. Dionne, A. Jornet, eds., *Doing CHAT in the Wild: From-the-Field Challenges of a Non-Dualist Methodology*, Vol. 7, Leiden: Koninklijke Brill NV. https://doi.org/10.1163/9789004548664_002.

Stetsenko, A. (2019b). Radical-transformative agency: Continuities and contrasts with relational agency and implications for education. *Learning,*

Culture and Social Interaction, 4, 1–13. https://doi.org/10.1016/j.lcsi.2018.04.002.

Stetsenko, A. (2021). Scholarship in the context of a historic socioeconomic and political turmoil: Commentary of Y. Engestrom and A. Sannino 'from mediated actions to heterogenous coalitions: Four generations of activity-theoretical studies of work and learning'. *Mind, Culture, and Activity* 28(1), 32–43. https://doi.org/10.1080/10749039.2021.1874419.

Stetsenko, A. (2020a). Transformative-activist and social justice approaches to the history of psychology. In W. E. Pickren, ed., *The Oxford Encyclopaedia of the History of Modern Psychology*. Oxford: Oxford University Press. https://api.semanticscholar.org/CorpusID:216371394.

Stetsenko, A., Bal, A., Choudry, S., Ferholt, B., Jornet, A., & Lemos, M. (2025). Reflections on the ISCAR 2024 Congress. *Mind, Culture, and Activity*, 54(5), 313–338. DOI: 10.1080/10749039.2025.2450002

Thelen, E. (2005). Dynamic systems theory and the complexity of change. *Psychoanalytic Dialogues*, 15(2), 255–283. https://doi.org/10.1080/10481881509348831.

Tutu, D. (2005). *God Has a Dream*. New York: Doubleday.

Van Ouers, B. (2015). Implementing a play-based curriculum: Fostering teacher agency in primary school. *Learning, Culture, and Social Interaction*, 4, 19–27. https://doi.org/10.1016/j.lcsi.2014.07.003.

Van Vlaenderen, H. (1999). Problem solving: A process of reaching common understanding and consensus. *South African Journal of Psychology*, 29(4), 166–177.

Van Waarmelo, N. J. (1989). *Venda Dictionary*. Pretoria: Government Printer.

Vianna, E., & Stetsenko, A. (2011). Connecting learning and identity development through a transformative activist stance: Application in adolescent development in a child welfare program. *Human Development*, 54(5), 313–338. https://doi.org/10.1159/000331484.

Vygotsky, L. S. (1997). The history of the development of higher mental functions. In R. W. Rieber, ed., *The Collected Works of L. S. Vygotsky*. New York: Plenum Press, pp. 1–252.

Vygotsky, L. S. (1978). *Mind in Society: The Development of Higher Psychological Processes*. Cambridge, MA: Harvard University Press.

Young, M. (2007). What are schools for? *Education and Society*, 28, 1287–1302. https://api.semanticscholar.org/.

Acknowledgements

I owe my gratitude for this Element, which I would not have been able to produce had it not been for the unwavering support of my family, Mpho, my lovely wife, in whom I derive strength to go on even when things seem impossible. My sons, Mufhu, Ndivhu, Thendo, and Teba – you have become my pillars of strength, standing by my side in all things. Mufhu has especially been very supportive throughout my writing and always lending a hand with all things digital.

I thank my my sisters Lydia and Florah, my only siblings who have been my de facto parents and have played such invaluable roles in my life, and my mulamu Willie Muthabi, always a father figure and perfect role model. I extend my gratitude to my late mother, Rahel. My father, Ramukhadi; Phophi, my aunt; Rambofheni, my uncle – all played such an indispensable role, especially since my own mother passed on quite early in my life.

My teachers, especially my primary school teacher whom my peers dubbed 'my mother at school', *Mme* Nemukongwe; my late pastor Ragimana, who often called me 'his son' and I called 'my father'; friends at school and in the villages when I grew up; and my peers at universities – all undoubtedly contributed immensely into my becoming. I also acknowledge my mother in law, Madiporo Maepa, for standing by my family – truly a mother indeed.

I have also benefited from many friends and colleagues at schools in Venda and Giyani where I worked briefly before joining the academy at the universities of the Witwatersrand, Cape Town, Pretoria, and Fort Hare. I am grateful to my colleagues in these universities, from whom I benefited immensely from vibrant conversations, robust debates and exchange of ideas about issues and problems of pedagogy within our schooling and society. I wish especially to thank Anna Stetsenko at the City University of New York. I have benefited immensely from the many years of unwavering support and the solidarity I enjoyed in an otherwise very lonely world of academy.

There are, of course, many more colleagues, friends and family who truly deserve mentioning had it not been for space limitation. To all these, I will truly always be indebted.

Finally, the teachers, students, and the community members: I benefited immensely from the generosity I received and here wish to express my sincere gratitude . I hope though, that you will agree with my interpretations, and where they may not be accurate to your meanings, I hope you will accept that it was not intended and that you will kindly forgive me as you have done many times in the past.

Last, but not least, I wish to acknowledge the grant from the National Research Fund (NRF) that enabled me to travel and exchange ideas related to the content of the current publication with colleagues abroad. However, NRF does not in any way necessarily endorse or support the ideas and views expressed in this publication, nor do all the persons mentioned above in this statement of acknowledgements.

Fhulufhelo Azwihangwisi Edward Muthivhi

Funding Acknowledgement

This work was funded by the National Research Foundation (NRF), Grant number: CPRR230522108772-PR-2024

Funding from the Department of Early Childhood Education, University of Pretoria, made it possible for this book to be published open access, making the digital version freely available for anyone to read and reuse under a Creative Commons licence.

Cambridge Elements

Critical Issues in Teacher Education

Tony Loughland
University of New South Wales
Tony Loughland is an Associate Professor in the School of Education at the University of New South Wales, Australia. Tony is currently leading projects on using AI for citizens' informed participation in urban development, the provision of staffing for rural and remote areas in NSW and on Graduate Ready Schools.

Andy Gao
University of New South Wales
Andy Gao is a Professor in the School of Education at the University of New South Wales, Australia. He edits various internationally-renowned journals, such as International Review of Applied Linguistics in Language Teaching for De Gruyter and Asia Pacific Education Researcher for Springer.

Hoa T. M. Nguyen
University of New South Wales
Hoa T. M. Nguyen is an Associate Professor in the School of Education at the University of New South Wales, Australia. She specializes in teacher education/development, mentoring and sociocultural theory.

Editorial Board
Megan Blumenreich, *CUNY*
Ricardo Cuenca, *Universidad Nacional Mayor de San Marcos, Peru*
Viv Ellis, *Monash University*
Declan Fahie, *UCD Dublin*
Amanda Gutierrez, *ACU Australia*
Jo Lampert, *Monash University*
Lily Orland-Barak, *University of Haifa*
Auli Toom, *University of Helsinki*
Simone White, *RMIT Australia*
Juhan Ye, *BNU China*
Hongbiao Yin, *Chinese University of Hong Kong*
Zhu Xhudong, *BNU China*

About the Series
This series addresses the critical issues teacher educators and teachers are engaged with in the increasingly complex profession of teaching. These issues reside in teachers' response to broader social, cultural and political shifts and the need for teachers' professional education to equip them to teach culturally and linguistically diverse students.

Cambridge Elements

Critical Issues in Teacher Education

Elements in the Series

Interculturality, Criticality and Reflexivity in Teacher Education
Fred Dervin

Enhancing Educators' Theoretical and Practical Understandings of Critical Literacy
Vera Sotirovska and Margaret Vaughn

Reclaiming the Cultural Politics of Teaching and Learning: Schooled in Punk
Greg Vass

Language Teacher's Social Cognition
Hao Xu

Who am I as a Teacher? Migrant Teachers' Redefined Professional Identity
Annika Käck

Professional Supervision for Principals: A Primer for Emerging Practice
Mary Ann Hunter and Geoff Broughton

Decolonizing Pedagogy in Post-Apartheid South Africa: A Post-Vygotskian Ethicopolitical and Ontoepistemic Postulation
Azwihangwisi Edward Muthivhi

A full series listing is available at: www.cambridge.org/EITE

For EU product safety concerns, contact us at Calle de José Abascal, 56–1°, 28003 Madrid, Spain or eugpsr@cambridge.org.

www.ingramcontent.com/pod-product-compliance
Lightning Source LLC
LaVergne TN
LVHW011853060526
838200LV00054B/4318